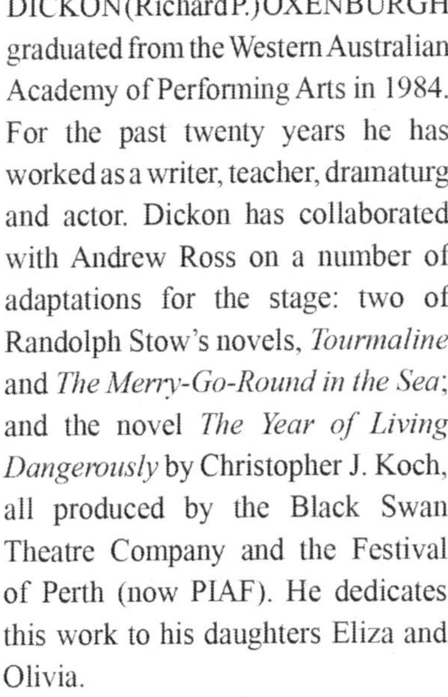

DICKON (Richard P.) OXENBURGH graduated from the Western Australian Academy of Performing Arts in 1984. For the past twenty years he has worked as a writer, teacher, dramaturg and actor. Dickon has collaborated with Andrew Ross on a number of adaptations for the stage: two of Randolph Stow's novels, *Tourmaline* and *The Merry-Go-Round in the Sea*; and the novel *The Year of Living Dangerously* by Christopher J. Koch, all produced by the Black Swan Theatre Company and the Festival of Perth (now PIAF). He dedicates this work to his daughters Eliza and Olivia.

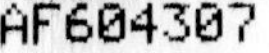

ANDREW ROSS has been Director of La Boite Theatre in Brisbane, the Melbourne University Theatre Department and Black Swan Theatre which he founded in 1991. He is currently Director of Brisbane Powerhouse. He has directed premieres of a number of significant Western Australian plays including *The Dreamers*, *No Sugar* and *Barungin* (by Jack Davis), *Meekatharra* (Lois Akimovich), *Sister girl* (Sally Morgan), *Bran Nue Dae* (Jimmy Chi and Kuckles), *Corrugation Road* (Jimmy Chi) and *Plainsong* (David Britton). He directed adaptations of *Midnite*, *Tourmaline* and *The Merry-Go-Round in the Sea*. He has taught and directed at the Western Australian Academy of Performing Arts and Victorian College for the Arts. His productions have toured to the UK and Canada and have won a number of awards including a Melbourne Greenroom Award and the Age Melbourne Critics' Award for Best Production.

THE MERRY-GO-ROUND IN THE SEA

The play

Dickon Oxenburgh & Andrew Ross

Adapted from the novel by

Randolph Stow

Currency Press, Sydney

CURRENCY PLAYS

First published in 2006
by Currency Press Pty Ltd,
PO Box 2287, Strawberry Hills, NSW, 2012, Australia
enquiries@currency.com.au
www.currency.com.au

The Merry-Go-Round in the Sea, the novel, by Randolph Stow, published by Penguin Books.

Reprinted 2012 (twice), 2014, 2017, 2021

NATIONAL LIBRARY OF AUSTRALIA CIP DATA

Oxenburgh, Dickon.

The Merry-go-round in the sea: the play.

ISBN 978 0 86819 788 3.

ISBN 0 86819 788 2.

1. Stow, Randolph, 1935– Merry-go-round in the sea. 2. National characteristics, Australian – Drama. 3. World War, 1939–1945 – Australia – Influence – Drama. I. Ross, Andrew Charles. II. Stow, Randolph, 1935– . III. Title.

A822.3

Australia Council for the Arts

Publication of this title was assisted by the Commonwealth Government through the Australia Council, its arts funding and advisory body.

Printed by Fineline Print & Copy Service, Revesby, NSW.
Cover design by Kate Florance, Currency Press.
Front cover shows Gemma Mylonas, Kathryn Hanlon and Brian Rooney 'on the road to Sandalwood' in the 1997 Black Swan Theatre Company production. Photo: Frances Andrijich. Back cover shows (from left) Murray Dowsett, Andrew Broadbent, Rosemary Barr, Trevor Jamieson, Elizabeth Spencer and Steve Saunders in the company's 2003 revival. Photo: Jurgen Lunsmann.

Contents

Foreword

Robert Juniper

I have been a fan of Randolph (or Mick as he is known to his friends) Stow's work since I was asked to design the covers for his books *To the Islands* and *Tourmaline*. I got to know him at this time, and subsequently designed the sets for three dramatisations of his books: *Tourmaline*, which is set in the Murchison, *Midnite* (great fun), and *The Merry-Go-Round in the Sea.*

The Merry-Go-Round in the Sea is set in Geraldton, Western Australia—Stow's birthplace—and I imagine it is partly autobiographical: about a young man's journey into adulthood. The merry-go-round itself is a sinking vessel. To a young boy, the mast and rigging forming a triangle protruding from the ocean would appear as a merry-go-round.

During my work on *Merry-Go-Round* I made several journeys to Geraldton, and it was from these trips that I was able to get a feel of where Stow was (literally) coming from. When one is driving there, the sunflowers start to appear along the fence lines at Greenough; Stow described them as Geraldton's 'weeds'. In my design of the set for *Merry-Go-Round*, I tried to give the impression of a sun-drenched landscape, with the sunflower theme prominent.

These same fence lines provide the backdrop for another of Stow's metaphors. The trees had been forced by the prevailing winds to abandon their natural vertical intent, and grow horizontally. To Rob Coram, the central character of *The Merry-Go-Round in the Sea*, they appeared as 'ladies washing their hair'. The reality of these tortured, distorted trees becomes such a gentle vision when seen through Stow's poetic eye.

I thoroughly enjoyed the experience of working on *The Merry-Go-Round in the Sea*. Stow handles his subject with warmth, vitality and keen observation, and the play is a fine adaptation of his charming and delightful story of a young man's life in Geraldton.

Robert Juniper is a Western Australian and studied commercial art and industrial design in England before returning to WA in 1949 to teach art. Since 1974, he has devoted himself full time to painting, sculpting and other forms of creative inventiveness. Juniper has established himself as one of Australia's leading painters, and is best known for his evocative depiction of the Western Australian landscape. He designed the set for Black Swan Theatre Company's 1997 production and 2003 revival of The Merry-Go-Round in the Sea.

The Merry-Go-Round in the Sea was first produced by Black Swan Theatre Company in association with the Western Australian Academy of Performing Arts at the Subiaco Theatre Centre, Perth, on 15 February 1997, with the following cast:

ROB CORAM	Brian Rooney
RICK MAPLESTEAD	Kim Delury
HUGH MACKAY / KEVIN / PATRICK	Michael Angus
GRAHAM / FRANK / RETURNED PRISONER OF WAR	Murray Dowsett
MARGARET CORAM	Kathryn Hanlon
MRS VINEGAR / LES / REG	Trevor Jamieson
MARY MAPLESTEAD / GIRL / GOLDIE THE HORSE	Raechelle Lee
AUNT KAY MACRAE / TEACHER	Caroline McKenzie
NAN CORAM	Gemma Mylonas
JANE WEXFORD / DIDI / AUNT ROSA / MR VINEGAR	Ingrid Ruz
AUNT MAY / GRANDMA MAPLESTEAD / SUSAN MAPLESTEAD	Elizabeth Spencer

Director, Andrew Ross
Set Design, Robert Juniper and Kim Saunders
Costume Design, Kim Saunders
Lighting Design, Duncan Ord
Original Music, Iain Grandage
Music performed by Magnetic Pig
Movement, Anna Mercer

CHARACTERS

ROB CORAM, a boy
MARGARET CORAM, Rob's mother
NAN CORAM, Rob's younger sister
GRANDMA MAPLESTEAD, Rob's grandmother
AUNT KAY MACRAE, Rob's great aunt
RICK MAPLESTEAD, Rob's older cousin
MARY MAPLESTEAD, Rick's mother
SUSAN MAPLESTEAD, Rick's sister
PATRICK, a young cousin
DIDI, a young cousin
JANE WEXFORD, Rick's fiancée
HUGH MACKAY, Rick's mate
JOY MACKAY, Hugh's wife
KEVIN, Rob's schoolmate
GRAHAM, Rob's schoolmate
FRANK, an old farmhand
RETURNED PRISONER OF WAR
MRS VINEGAR, a fairytale character
MR VINEGAR, a fairytale character
LES, a teenage boy
REG, a young soldier
TOM, Reg's mate
SCHOOLGIRL
PRIMARY SCHOOL TEACHER

ACT ONE

RICK AWAY 1941–1945

SCENE ONE

THE MERRY-GO-ROUND

A Murchison landscape sweeps across the stage.

The performance area is thrust-style with a cyclorama landscape across the back of the stage. The colours are earth, gold and sky. A series of ramps traverse the landscape, so figures can move across its painterly surface. In the centre of the stage is a large revolve, which is used to segue from scene to scene. On the left edge of the stage stands a corrugated tank that serves as a pool and, to the right, the musicians' area. The CHORUS *takes up position on the ramps, in the landscape.*

ROB *lies in the middle of the revolve—in the grass—his eyes closed to the sun. He begins to count out the seconds to a minute. Music begins. The* CHORUS *speaks over* ROB*'s counting.*

ROB: One, two, three, four…
CHORUS: The merry-go-round…
ROB: … five, six, seven, eight…
CHORUS: The merry-go-round had a centre post of cast iron…
ROB: … nine, ten, eleven, twelve…
CHORUS: … reddened a little by the salt air, and of a certain ornateness.
ROB: … thirteen, fourteen, fifteen, sixteen…
CHORUS: The post began as a square pillar, formed rings…
ROB: … seventeen, eighteen, nineteen…
CHORUS: … continued as a fluted column…
ROB: … twenty, twenty-one, twenty-two…
CHORUS: … suddenly bulged like a diseased tree with an excrescence of iron leaves…
ROB: … twenty-three, twenty-four, twenty-five…
CHORUS: … narrowed to the peak like the top of a pepper pot…

ROB: … twenty-six, twenty-seven, twenty-eight, twenty-nine, thirty…

CHORUS: … ending very high in the sky with an iron ball.
In the bulge where the leaves were, was an iron collar.

ROB: … thirty-one, thirty-two, thirty-three, thirty-four, thirty-five…

CHORUS: From this collar eight iron stays hung down…

ROB: … thirty-six, thirty-seven, thirty-eight, thirty-nine, forty…

CHORUS: … supporting the narrow, wooden octagonal seat of the merry-go-round.

ROB: … forty-one, forty-two, forty-three, forty-four, forty-five…

CHORUS: The planks were polished by the bottoms of children.

ROB: … forty-six, forty-seven, forty-eight, forty-nine, fifty…

CHORUS: And on every one of the stays was a small unrusted section…

ROB: … fifty-one, fifty-two, fifty-three, fifty-four, fifty-five…

CHORUS: … where the hands of the adults had sent the merry-go-round spinning!

ROB: … fifty-six, fifty-seven, fifty-eight, fifty-nine, sixty!
That is a minute. It will never be that minute again.
It will never be today again. Never.

MARGARET *appears as the* CHORUS *forms a merry-go-round on the revolve.*

MARGARET: Rob—Rob Coram!

CHORUS: [*echoing*] Rob—Rob Coram!

ROB: Here I am, Mummy.

MARGARET: You're a naughty boy, I told you to stay in the car!

ROB: I want a ride on the merry-go-round.

MARGARET: We haven't got time. We're going to pick up Nan from Grandma and Aunt Kay's.

ROB: I want a ride!

MARGARET: [*giving in*] Don't scowl at me, Rob.

ROB: Lift me up.

MARGARET: [*lifting him onto the merry-go-round*] Oof!—You're getting heavy.

ROB: Aunt Kay lets me ride on her back and she's old.

MARGARET: Aunt Kay is very naughty. You mustn't let her give you piggy-backs.

ROB: You're not as strong as Aunt Kay.

MARGARET: Do you want a ride?

Rob on the the merry-go-round (from left): Trevor Jamieson, Brian Rooney as Rob Coram and Murray Dowsett in Black Swan Theatre Company's 1997 production. (Photo: Frances Andrijich)

ROB: Yes—push me faster!

MARGARET: Oh, Rob, it's too hot.

ROB: Why don't you run round with it like Mavis does?

MARGARET: It's too hot. That's enough, we must go now.

ROB: Mavis made it go fast. She ran with it.

MARGARET: Mavis is a young girl.

ROB: Why did Mavis go away?

MARGARET: To get married.

ROB: Why don't we have another maid?

MARGARET: People don't have maids now.

ROB: Why don't people have maids?

MARGARET: Because of the war. People don't have maids in wartime.

ROB: Are the Japanese wicked?

MARGARET: They're the enemy.

ROB: Wickeder than the Germans?

MARGARET: They did something very wicked. They dropped bombs on Pearl Harbour.

ROB: Is Pearl Harbour like Geraldton?

MARGARET: I suppose, a bit…

ROB: It must be a place like Geraldton—everyone is always talking about it.

MARGARET: [*stops pushing*] That's enough, it's too hot. Come along, quick sticks, we're going to Grandma's house.

She goes to drag him off.

ROB: Mummy?

MARGARET: Yes, Rob?

ROB: Can't I go to the merry-go-round in the sea? Just once?

MARGARET: Oh, Rob, won't you ever believe me? There's no merry-go-round in the sea.

ROB: It looks like a merry-go-round in the sea. It must be a merry-go-round in the sea.

MARGARET: It's a big boat. It's a big sort of barge that was carting rocks to build the breakwater. And one night there was a storm, and it sank. What you can see is the mast and the iron things that hold the mast up. It just happens to look like a merry-go-round.

She starts to leave. He follows, dawdling behind her.

ROB: Have you been there?

MARGARET: Yes, I've seen it.

ROB: Well, can't I go, then? Can't I go there with you?

MARGARET: No, we can't, Rob. We can't go there.

ROB: Why? Why can't we go there?

MARGARET: Oh—because of the war. Darling, you know that that end of the beach is where Daddy's camp is, and no one can go there now except the garrison. There are barbed-wire fences there to keep people out. So we can't go to the merry-go-round—I mean the wreck—not till after the war. But you'll go there someday, if you really want to see it. The war won't last forever.

ROB: [*defiantly*] When I'm big I'll *swim* out to the merry-go-round in the sea, I'll swim miles and miles until I get to the merry-go-round fixed in the sea and I'll bring Rick too, and Aunt Kay, and we'll stay there always, with the world turning around us, spinning, and nothing will change and it will be today forever.

MARGARET: Rob, come on.

They start to walk.

ROB: Mummy, why aren't I Japanese?

MARGARET: What?

ROB: Why aren't I Japanese? There are millions of them and only a few of us.

MARGARET: Come along, Grandma's expecting us.

ROB: Mummy, is Geraldton old?

MARGARET: Oh, very old.

ROB: Older than Australia?

MARGARET: Australia's a young country.

ROB: But it's old too, older than the Depression, older than anything… I think it was asleep like Sleeping Beauty. Mummy, if everyone left town would the sand come back?

MARGARET: I suppose so.

ROB: And bury it?

MARGARET: I suppose so.

ROB: Would it be like snow?

MARGARET: Rob!

ROB: Then there would be no town at all, just white sandhills.

MARGARET: For goodness sake, get a move on, Rob Coram.

ROB: I am Rob Coram, I live in Geraldton. Rob Coram, Rob Coram, Rob Coram…

♦♦♦♦♦

SCENE TWO

GRANDMA'S HOUSE

A strange sight—GRANDMA *(Mrs Maplestead) washing her hair in a basin.*

ROB: Grandma Maplestead's house was an old station homestead sitting in a town. This was because to Mrs Maplestead, and to Aunt Kay (Mrs MacKay MacRae), her sister and to the late Charles Maplestead, her husband, a house meant a homestead and nothing less. The house had a garden. At some point in the past load upon load of rich loam had come from one of Charles MacRae's farms, pockets of red sand had embedded in the sand and things grew. But the best thing in the garden had been there always. It was the giant Moreton Bay fig tree that arched over the stone house dropping its dried fruits clatter, clatter on the iron roof. The flowers of the white oleander beside the gate were withered and browned by the hot easterly that blew in the mornings and, in the heat, the bigger flowers of the red oleander smelled overwhelmingly, sickeningly sweet…

He is about to sample some.

MARGARET: Don't put that in your mouth, you silly boy—it's poisonous.

ROB *crosses to* GRANDMA *who is now drying her hair.*

ROB: Grandma and Aunt Kay are always washing their hair. Look, a lady with no face…

He sings.

Queen Anne, Queen Anne, you sit in the sun,
As fair as a lily, as white as a wand.
I send you three letters, I pray you read one.

GRANDMA: Is that you, Rob? Cheeky thing. Is Mummy there?

MARGARET: Yes.

GRANDMA: Oh, hullo!

She sits down and brushes her hair. ROB *strokes it.*

ROB: You've got a nice face and nice white hair, Grandma. It's very long, isn't it? When it's not in a bun. What's that smell?

GRANDMA: That's ammonia.

ROB: Pneumonia? Why are you washing your hair in pneumonia?
MARGARET: Rob!
ROB: Why have you got spots on your hands?
MARGARET: Rob!
GRANDMA: Because I'm old. Are you going to Sandalwood, then?
MARGARET: I suppose so. I'd love a cup of tea.
GRANDMA: Well, there's time.
ROB: Grandma, where's Aunt Kay?
GRANDMA: She's in the playroom with your sister Nan.
ROB: Oh.
GRANDMA: Can you whistle yet, Rob?
ROB: No, I haven't got my front teeth.
GRANDMA: Say 'six thick thistle sticks'.
ROB: No. That's silly. I'm going to talk to Aunt Kay.

Grandma's house was really two houses. At the front there was a house for living, which was convict-built out of stone with massive walls and small, dark rooms. And at the back was a wooden house composed of store rooms, among them an apple room, where big yellow-green granny smith apples lay about on the table smelling sweetly. Big, black preserving pans hung in the pantry, which smelled of spice, and onions, and stifling heat.

ROB *walks through to find* AUNT KAY, *sitting on a stool, mending socks.* ROB *trips over* NAN.

NAN: Waaaaa!
AUNT KAY: Oh, Jeff!… I mean, Gordon!… I mean—Rob!
ROB: Sorry, Nan. [*Aside*] Nan is four and beneath contempt. [*To* AUNT KAY] What are you doing, Aunt Kay?
AUNT KAY: Making a wigwam for a goose's bridle.
ROB: No, really.
AUNT KAY: A triantiwantigong.
ROB: No, really.
AUNT KAY: I'm darning men's socks.
ROB: You're always darning men's socks!
AUNT KAY: That's right. And when I'm not darning men's socks, I'm knitting socks or picking grass seeds out of socks or asking for news of the socks in outlying parts of the family. I go about the entire Maplestead clan, all the cousins, soliciting socks, and at the moment I'm darning a khaki sock.

ROB: That's one of Daddy's garrison socks.

AUNT KAY: No, it's one of Rick's.

ROB: Oh, is that Rick's? We're going to Sandalwood. We'll see Rick. He's going in the army.

AUNT KAY: Yes, that will be nice. I hope he'll come and say goodbye to all of us before he goes.

ROB: He'll have to come—to get his socks.

ROB *has been rummaging through Aunt Kay's sewing basket and has found a handful of thimbles, which he places on his fingers and then drums a tune on* NAN*'s head.*

NAN: Aunt Kaaay!

AUNT KAY: Rob!

ROB: I know you're not really cross with me, because I'm a boy.

AUNT KAY: Get away with you! Bring some water in.

ROB *takes wood and water to and from the water tank. He draws a bucketful of water, then stops, fascinated by his reflection. He dips his head in. He walks back and drips the water on* NAN. NAN *screams.*

NAN: Rob!

She bites him on the leg. ROB *kicks back.*

Muuumm!

MARGARET: Rob, did you kick Nan?

ROB: She bit me!

MARGARET: What did you do to make her bite you?

ROB: I dripped water on her, that's all. That didn't hurt her.

MARGARET: How did you get wet?

ROB: I put my head in the washing water.

MARGARET: Rob Corum, you're not to do that—you'll fall in and drown. Now get in the car. We're going to Sandalwood to see Rick.

The revolving stage brings on a tricycle, which represents a motor car. MARGARET, ROB *and* NAN *clamber aboard,* MARGARET *peddling.*

♦♦♦♦♦

SCENE THREE

JOURNEY TO SANDALWOOD

CHORUS: They passed the empty shops with dirty windows and houses with falling fences, sunflowers, Moreton Bay figs, purple bougainvillea glowing against the blue sea; they passed the old courthouse crumbling away, and Wainwright's store, where the early ships had landed supplies, that too was crumbling, like the bougainvillea-torn shed, like the upturned boat on the foreshore with sunflowers blossoming through its ribs.

They passed the familiar gum trees of Greenough, crippled and stooped by the Southerly, bowing northward and trailing their weeping leaves upon the ground. Rob knew for certain that he lived in an old land, in a haunted land.

MARGARET: Do you remember what you used to call those trees, Robbie?

ROB: Aw, ladies washing their hair. Can we go to the pool, Mummy? Can we please?

MARGARET: Not today, we're going to see Rick.

ROB: Just for a minute?

MARGARET: No.

ROB: [*sulkily*] You used to play there… Is it bottomless? There are bunyips in there, you know. They've been in there forever. Because it's the oldest thing in Australia.

MARGARET: Oh, Rob.

NAN: Mummy, when will we be there?

MARGARET: Soon.

NAN: When you count to how many?

MARGARET: When you count to a thousand.

NAN: One, two, three, four, five…

ROB: Oh, shut up.

MARGARET: Rob!

ROB: Well, she doesn't have to count out loud!

MARGARET: Don't you ever say shut up to your sister!

ROB: Sister. Huh.

The CHORUS *forms a flock of white cockatoos, wheeling and screeching over the car.*

NAN: Oh, look.

Above: Chorus of cockatoos (from left): Elizabeth Spencer, Gemma Mylonas as Nan Coram, Kathryn Hanlon as Margaret Coram, Brian Rooney as Rob Coram, Michael Angus and Raechelle Lee. Below: Kim Delury as Rick Maplestead and Brian Rooney as Rob Coram. Black Swan Theatre Company's 1997 production. (Photos: Frances Andrijich)

ROB: You're slow, I saw them ages ago.

MARGARET: Don't be disagreeable, Rob.

ROB: Oh, we're in Rick's country now. Mummy, will I sleep in Rick's room?

MARGARET: I don't know. That depends on Rick.

ROB: I want to!

MARGARET: I expect you will. But you're not to be a nuisance to Rick.

ROB: I'm not a nuisance.

MARGARET: But you're only a little boy and Rick's a grown-up man.

ROB: Is Rick a grown-up man?

MARGARET: He's nearly twenty-one.

ROB: [*wickedly*] He's nearly as old as you are.

MARGARET: [*smiling*] Cheeky thing!

RICK *appears, leading horses across one of the ramps.*

ROB: Look! There's Rick.

NAN: Where's Rick?

ROB: There. There.

MARGARET: He must be bringing in Goldie, so you can ride.

NAN: Oh, goody.

ROB: You can't ride.

MARGARET: She can so ride, if she wants to.

ROB: Well, she can't hold the reins.

MARGARET: Nor could you, when you were four.

ROB: I could so!

MARGARET: You don't even remember!

ROB: I do so remember!

MARGARET: Don't contradict.

They stop at the gate.

ROB: I'll get the gate. Do I close it?

MARGARET: Leave it the way you found it.

ROB: [*starting to run*] I'll race you then.

Music builds as ROB *runs against the revolve whilst the car goes on ahead to Sandalwood.*

♦♦♦♦♦

SCENE FOUR

ROB AND RICK

CHORUS: Past the tall palm trees and under the olives and behind the trellis of climbing roses lay a pool. In the little pond three waterlilies were flowering—their smooth lily leaves open to their yellow hearts.

ROB *enters and runs straight to the pond.*

ROB: [*sighing*] Oh.

MARGARET *and* NAN *are greeted by* SUSAN *and* AUNT MARY.

AUNT MARY: But didn't you bring Rob?
MARGARET: Oh, he's there, he's gone to find the lilies.
SUSAN: I don't like that pool. I'm always afraid the smaller ones will fall in.
AUNT MARY: Well, perhaps we should have it filled. Really, it does nothing but breed mosquitoes.
MARGARET: Rob, it's not polite to hide from Aunt Mary!

ROB *tears himself away from the pool.*

ROB: Hullo, Aunt Mary. We saw Rick. He was bringing in the horses.
AUNT MARY: I expect he was getting Goldie, for you children.
ROB: Are they going to ride?
SUSAN: Patrick is. Aren't you, Patrick?
PATRICK [*eating dirt*] What?
AUNT MARY: Look! Susan! Look!
SUSAN: Oh, lord.
ROB: He'll get sand. He'll die.
MARGARET: Don't be silly. Only horses get sand.

She watches SUSAN *with* PATRICK.

Poor Susan, three of that age.
AUNT MARY: The baby's wet too.
MARGARET: Shall I take him? Come along.
NAN: I want to do wee-wee.

They all exit except ROB. RICK *and Goldie revolve on.* RICK *is grooming and saddling the horse.* RICK *grabs* ROB *and tries to mess his hair with a horse brush.*

RICK: Hey, it's my younger cousin coming to get his hair done!
ROB: [*laughing*] Don't, don't, Rick!
RICK: Well, where have you been?
ROB: Home.
RICK: You didn't come and see me. I had your swag laid out on the bed, and you didn't come.
ROB: I've come now.
RICK: It's too late. You've hurt my feelings.
ROB: Oh, bulldust!
RICK: Hey, who taught you to say that?
ROB: You did.
RICK: Did I? You ever hear me talk like that, Goldie?
ROB: She has. She nodded.
RICK: She's a lying bitch.
ROB: [*laughing*] You shouldn't say that.
RICK: Ah, but you won't tell, will you?
ROB: When I swear Grandma puts mustard on my tongue.
RICK: Does she do that? Your grandma's a fierce old lady.

ROB *giggles.*

If everyone thought I was as funny as you do, I could go on the pictures and make a million dollars.
ROB: You're just goofy.
RICK: Well, this won't get the old girl's hair tidy.

He goes back to brushing Goldie.

ROB: How old is Goldie, Rick?
RICK: Old. Susan had her, then I had her when I was your age.
ROB: Really?
RICK: Fish the blanket out, will you?

ROB *gets the saddle blanket and smells it.*

ROB: It smells like—horse.
RICK: Aren't you a little wit. Well, do you want a ride?
ROB: Yes.
RICK: Yes, what?
ROB: Yes, Rick, I want a ride.
RICK: Right. Now you remember how to hold the reins? Loop them in your right hand and use your fingers to separate them.

ROB: They're still too small.
RICK: Never mind, use both hands, then.

He lifts ROB *onto the horse formed by three actors.*

Wow, you're getting heavy.
ROB: I'm six.
RICK: Are you really six? Then why aren't you in the army?
ROB: I'm going in the navy when I'm seven.
RICK: Come along, little wit, you can walk behind.
CHORUS: The hairs on the back of Rick's neck were golden. Two crows were crying in the sky, and everything was asleep. The day, the summer, would never end. He would walk behind Rick. He would study him forever.

♦♦♦♦♦

SCENE FIVE

TENNIS PARTY

Pong! A tennis ball sallies forth. A Sandalwood tennis game ensues centre stage, whilst benches are set up, that later become a bed.

ROB: In summer everyone played tennis, and in winter they played golf. Everybody's houses were full of silver cups and silver spoons for playing tennis and golf.
MARGARET: Game, set and match!
RICK: Margaret and I might win the cup again this year, what do you think, Mother?
AUNT MARY: I wish you wouldn't, I get sick of polishing them.
ROB: Stacks on the mill, more on still!

He leaps on RICK.

RICK: Hey, kid, fair go!

NAN *piles on, then the other children.*

Help me, Margaret, help me.
SUSAN: Children, don't bother Rick.
RICK: Oh boy, you give me a rough life.
ROB: You're rough.
RICK: [*baring his stomach*] Go on hit me, come on hit me!

ROB: [*punching him*] Gosh.
RICK: Now let me hit you!
ROB: No bloody fear!
MARGARET: Rob! Did you say that word?
ROB: What word?
MARGARET: That thing you say. You know what I mean.
RICK: He said: 'Come over here'.
MARGARET: Oh, Rick, you're worse than Mother and Aunt Kay.
AUNT MARY: I think Grandma should put mustard on his tongue.
ROB: I like mustard.
MARGARET: Are we going to play another set?
RICK: Not me, I reckon I've earned a beer.

All exit except MARGARET, ROB *and* FRANK. ROB *notices* FRANK, *near the water tank, carving something out of wood.*

ROB: Mum, who does Frank belong to?
MARGARET: He's not really related to anyone. But everyone loves him. He's been here for as long as I can remember, he was here when I was a child.
ROB: How did he get here?
MARGARET: When he was nine, he walked from Perth to Sandalwood, a whole three hundred miles. And he just stayed. Then he taught himself to read by reading the labels on jam tins.

ROB *is awed to silence by* FRANK.

Dinnertime and bedtime soon!

♦♦♦♦♦

SCENE SIX

ROB'S BEDTIME STORY

ROB *prepares for bed.* MARGARET *tucks him in.*

ROB: Mother, make my bed soon,
For I'm weary with the hunting,
And I fain would lie doon.
MARGARET: Cheeky thing!
ROB: Can Rick read to me?

MARGARET: We-ell, you've had all day with Rick, and he wants to talk with the grown-ups now.

ROB: Will you ask him?

MARGARET: Oh, all right. Goodnight.

RICK *enters eating an apple.*

RICK: I've been told to read to you. What'll it be? How about Dicey on the Law of the Constitution?

ROB: I've got a book.

RICK: Mmm... 'The Adventures of Mr and Mrs Vinegar'.

MR *and* MRS VINEGAR *appear.*

ROB: I love Mr and Mrs Vinegar.

RICK: Right. Here goes. The story of Mr and Mrs Vinegar. One day Mr Vinegar said to Mrs Vinegar...

MR VINEGAR: We must go on a journey, Mrs Vinegar, we must go to market.

MRS VINEGAR: Yes, Mr Vinegar. Our old red cow is dead, and we must go to market to buy a new cow, so that we shall have milk and butter and cream and cheese for our supper.

RICK: Some diet... I bet they weighed a ton.

MR VINEGAR: It's a very long way to market.

MRS VINEGAR: Yes, Mr Vinegar, and tonight I shall bake some bread, so that we shall have fresh bread and cheese for the journey.

ROB: So Mrs Vinegar baked her bread, and in the morning Mr and Mrs Vinegar rose very early, and wrapped the bread and the big red cheese in a fresh white cloth and prepared to go on their journey.

MRS VINEGAR: We must lock the door, Mr Vinegar, because of robbers.

MR VINEGAR: Yes, Mrs Vinegar. We must lock the door so that robbers may not come into our house and steal our big red cheeses.

RICK: So Mr and Mrs Vinegar locked their big green door, which Mr Vinegar had freshly painted on the previous Friday, and prepared to go to market. Just then Mrs Vinegar stopped and said:

MRS VINEGAR: Mr Vinegar?

MR VINEGAR: Yes, Mrs Vinegar?

MRS VINEGAR: If the robbers wish to steal our big red cheeses, they will break down our big green freshly-painted door.

The tone changes.

RICK: Mr Vinegar considered what Mrs Vinegar had said, and at last he said:

MR VINEGAR: Mrs Vinegar.

MRS VINEGAR: Yes, Mr Vinegar?

MR VINEGAR: I have heard that robbers are very wild and rough, and I fear that they will break our big green door even if it is open.

RICK *starts dressing in his army uniform.*

RICK: Mrs Vinegar considered what Mr Vinegar had said, and her heart grew heavy. Then suddenly Mrs Vinegar smiled.

MRS VINEGAR: Mr Vinegar.

MR VINEGAR: Yes, Mrs Vinegar?

MRS VINEGAR: Let us take our big green door, from its big black hinges, and carry it with us to market, and then it cannot be broken!

MR VINEGAR: You are a wise woman, Mrs Vinegar.

RICK: And together they lifted the big green door, from its big black hinges, and tied it to Mr Vinegar's back with a big white rope, and set out on their journey.

♦ ♦ ♦ ♦ ♦

Ingrid Ruz as Mr Vinegar and Trevor Jamieson as Mrs Vinegar in Black Swan Theatre Company's 1997 production. (Photo: Frances Andrijich)

SCENE SEVEN

RICK'S DEPARTURE

RICK *has completed dressing.*

ROB: Those are your soldier's clothes.
RICK: Yup. Do they make me look brave?
ROB: Are you going now, Rick?
RICK: I'm afraid so, kid.
ROB: Where are you going?
RICK: Well, I couldn't say. The big boys don't tell me their secrets.
ROB: Is it in Australia?
RICK: I don't know. It's a secret.

RICK *looks into an imaginary mirror and combs his hair. He is fascinated by his image as a soldier.*

ROB: I wish—I wish—

He starts to well up with tears.

RICK: Hey, fella, don't do that. I don't like to see a man cry like that, with real tears. If a man's got to cry he'd do better to bawl his head off.
ROB: I'm not crying.
RICK: And I'll be back. I'll be back and all you'll be able to see will be two eyes peering through gongs and fruit salad.
ROB: I wish you didn't have to.
RICK: Well, I do.
ROB: I wish it wasn't today.
RICK: But you knew I was going. That's why you came, to say goodbye.
ROB: I want to say goodbye now. Here.
RICK: Well, goodbye.
ROB: Goodbye.

ROB *cries.*

RICK: Oh, kid. Baby. It's all right.
ROB: I know. I know. I just wish it wasn't today.

ROB *kisses* RICK.

♦♦♦♦♦

SCENE EIGHT

ROB'S WAR

RICK *vanishes into the chorus of Maplesteads and Corums.*

CHORUS: The boy's life had no progression, his days led nowhere. He woke in the morning in his room, and at night he slept: the wheel turning full circle, the merry-go-round of his life revolving.

AUNT KAY: Blood! Blood! He saw on every side!
But nowhere found the child!

CHORUS: Poems did not make him laugh or cry or anything, but were simply magic. Words possessed his mind: a meaningless magic, a land of snow.

ROB: Grey goose and gander
Waft your wings together
Carry the good King's daughter
Over the one-strand river…

Aunt Kay, why aren't there any poems about black swans?

CHORUS: [*singing 'In the Bleak Midwinter'*]
In the bleak midwinter, frosty wind made moan,
Earth stood hard as iron, water like a stone;
Snow had fallen, snow on snow, snow on snow,
In the bleak midwinter, long ago.

His days revolved, they moved towards no culmination. His mother turned out the light and he lay in the dark. At night, the windmill clanked in the sky and the sea roared to the southward. The sea moaned through his childhood, a morning sighing, thumping in winter rains. In the country, trees took the place of the sea, trees sighed him to sleep. But the sea-sound to which he was born was the first sound, the beginning and ending of all his circling days.

ROB *prepares for bed.* AUNT KAY *begins to recite a poem.* ROB *falls asleep. She exits and the poem continues as a chorus of 'nasty nightgowns' appears.*

A man of words and not of deeds
Is like a garden full of weeds,

And when the weeds begin to blow
It's like a garden full of snow,

And when the snow begins to fall
It's like a bird upon the wall,

And when the bird begins to fly
It's like an eagle in the sky,

And when the sky begins to roar
It's like a lion at your door,

And when the door begins to crack
It's like a stick across your back…

ROB: Get away!

CHORUS: And when your back begins to smart
It's like a penknife in your heart,

And when your heart begins to bleed
You're dead, and dead, and dead indeed.

ROB: [*screaming*] Get away, you nasty old nightgowns!

The nightmares vanish. MARGARET *enters and comforts* ROB.

In the distance New Year celebrations, and the sounds of 'Auld Lang Syne'.

MARGARET: What's the matter, Rob? Did you have a nasty?

ROB: No. It's the noises.

MARGARET: Oh, that's the grown-ups being silly. The ships are blowing their sirens and people are tooting their car horns because it's New Year.

ROB: What's New Year?

MARGARET: Well, it's a different year from last year, with a different number. Yesterday it was 1941 and today it's 1942.

ROB: A happy New Year? Mummy, 1941 was a sad year when Rick went away. Now we're going to be happy and Rick will come back again, because there's only one place to be happy, and that's here.

MARGARET: Happy New Year, Robbie.

ROB: Happy New Year, Mummy.

AUNT KAY *enters.* ROB *grows sleepy again.*

Aunt Kay, sing 'Lord Randall'.

AUNT KAY: How you love 'Lord Randall'! I don't really think it's a song for little boys, but still…

Where have you been a roving, John Randolph, my son?
Where have you been a roving, John Randolph, my son?
Pray tell me, little one.

I've been out a courting. Go make my bed soon.
Mother, I'm sick in the heart and I want to lie down.

What will you will to your sweetheart, John Randolph, my son?
Pray tell me, little one.

A cup of strong poison. Go make my bed soon.
Mother, I'm sick in the heart and I want to lie down.

ROB: Did you sing 'Lord Randall' to Rick?

AUNT KAY: I don't remember, I expect so. He and Susan were often here, with the girls.

ROB: Where is Rick now?

AUNT KAY: I don't really know, Rob. Poor wee lad.

ROB: Who? Rick?

AUNT KAY: He's far from home and it's his twenty-first birthday.

ROB: Is it Rick's birthday? Did you send him a present?

AUNT KAY: Oh, no. But when he comes home we'll give him one. We'll give him one for every birthday he's missed.

ROB: Will he miss many birthdays?

AUNT KAY: I really don't know.

AUNT KAY *exits*. MARGARET *appears*.

ROB: Can you read me a story, Mummy?

MARGARET: One day Mr Vinegar said to Mrs Vinegar…

MR VINEGAR: We must go on a journey, Mrs Vinegar. We must go to market.

MRS VINEGAR: Yes, Mr Vinegar. Our old red cow is dead, and we must go to market to buy a new cow, so that we shall have milk, and butter, and cream, and cheese for our supper.

ROB: Rick laughed at that. He said it was mad.

MARGARET: Well, don't you think it was mad?

ROB: Oh, ye-es. They should have stayed at home.

MARGARET: But then they wouldn't have got all the gold when their door fell out of the tree on top of the robbers.

ROB: But they didn't need the gold. They had all that cheese.

MARGARET: Oh, you unadventurous old thing!

ROB: It's Rick's birthday.

MARGARET: So it is.

Leonard Goulds as Rob Coram and Kirsty Hillhouse as Margaret Coram in Black Swan Theatre Company's 2003 production. (Photo: Jurgen Lunsmann)

ROB: Aunt Kay told me.
MARGARET: Aren't you and Aunt Kay a pair of old gossips?
ROB: Aunt Kay doesn't know where Rick is. Where is he, Mummy?
MARGARET: Come on, let's get on with Mr and Mrs Vinegar.
ROB: [*suspiciously*] Where is he?

Rising tension.

MARGARET: Mrs Vinegar considered what Mr Vinegar had said and her heart grew weary. Then suddenly she smiled.
ROB: Where is he?
MRS VINEGAR: Mr Vinegar.
MARGARET: I don't know, Rob. Let's—
MR VINEGAR: Yes, Mrs Vinegar?
MRS VINEGAR: Let us take our big green door…
ROB: Where is he, Mummy?
MARGARET: Don't raise your voice to me!
MRS VINEGAR: … from its big black hinges.
MARGARET: He's in Malaya.

♦♦♦♦♦

SCENE NINE

THE RAILWAY

The door on a different, fiery world is thrown open. The elongated shadow of a man appears. RICK, *covered in blood, steps forward and falls down. The dim outline of another man,* HUGH, *can be seen, slumped against a wall.*

HUGH: Okay? You all right? Hey, mate… That's blood… Hey, what did they do? Are you hurt?
RICK: Not mine, not mine.
HUGH: What happened? Are you hurt?
RICK: I'll live.
HUGH: The blood—
RICK: I don't know his name. We were tied together. They cut his head off.
HUGH: Oh, Christ!
RICK: He said, 'Sport, we can't be worried'.

HUGH: You, what about you?

RICK: I'll live.

HUGH: You need help?

No answer.

Listen, listen do something for me?

RICK: Yes?

HUGH: You a 'Groper too?

RICK: Yes.

HUGH: If the torch shines on me, or one of the firing squads finally fires, and you get back—tell the folks…

RICK: Yes?

HUGH: Hugh MacKay. Midland Junction.

RICK: I'll remember.

HUGH: What about you? What's your name?

RICK: Richard Maplestead. Geraldton.

HUGH: Got it.

RICK: This is my twenty-first. I've come of age.

HUGH: I hope you've had a very happy day. Hey, you horrible little bastards! A man here wants a key to the door!

An atmosphere of ominous confusion as MARGARET *tries to soothe* ROB.

♦♦♦♦♦

SCENE TEN

ROB'S WAR

The CHORUS *echoes above air-raid sirens.*

CHORUS: Singapore. Batavia. Surabaya. Darwin. Broome.

ROB: Why are they talking about Broome?

MARGARET: Who is talking about Broome?

ROB: Does Broome belong to the Japs?

MARGARET: No. And it never will.

ROB: *Why* are they talking about it?

MARGARET: Oh, if you must know, the Japs have dropped some bombs there.

ROB: [*frightened*] Then they're coming.

MARGARET: No. No, don't be silly, Rob. The Japs can't come to Australia. God wouldn't let them.

ROB: Why wouldn't he if Rick lets them drop bombs on Broome? Mummy, where's Daddy?

MARGARET: He's in the garrison.

ROB: He's always in the garrison. Mum, what are those things on the water? Are they boats or aeroplanes?

MARGARET: They're Catalinas.

ROB: Flying boats! Gee! Why have they painted the wheat bins funny colours?

MARGARET: It's camouflage, Rob, so the Japs won't see them.

ROB: Do the Japs want to wreck our wheat bins?

ROB *notices a man digging.*

Mummy, why is that man digging a hole?

MARGARET: It's a trench.

ROB: What for?

MARGARET: It's an air-raid trench.

ROB: What's an air-raid trench?

MARGARET: Well, it's a hole in the tennis court, and we have to sit in it sometimes. Just in case the Japs drop bombs.

MARGARET *exits.*

ROB: On *us*? Drop *bombs* on us?

He puts on an army helmet.

The CHORUS *circle around* ROB *as an air-raid siren wails. He is now under the table. He wakes and screams.* MARGARET *and* AUNT KAY *rush in and pull him out from under the table.*

AUNT KAY: Rob, it's all right. It's all right.

ROB: Coffin… I was in a coffin.

MARGARET: We put you under the table while you were sleeping. It's all right. Shhh.

ROB: Everything's changed.

AUNT KAY: Everything will be as it always has.

MARGARET: It's all right, darling.

Two CHORUS *members come on, pick up the table-top and bench with* ROB *on it and start to carry him off.* NAN *enters with a suitcase and teddy bear. They all start packing up.*

ROB: What's happening?
GRANDMA: We're evacuating.
ROB: What's evacuating?
AUNT KAY: It's a funny word for we're all going to Sandalwood!
ROB: [*cheering*] Sandalwood!

♦♦♦♦♦

SCENE ELEVEN

EVACUATION

The stage revolves them around to Sandalwood. AUNT MARY *has secateurs in hand,* SUSAN *is pushing a pram.*

CHORUS: The Easter lilies had opened, their delicate pink throats had opened around dusty stamens. A clean, clean sweetness was about them. They had no leaves. Red stems rose clean from the hard ground. Lilies and oranges and roses. Each scent was distinct in the late summer garden. Pepper trees smelled sharp, like ants. Berries lay on the ground, beads of dry, red lacquer.

FRANK *and* ROB *exchange a quiet moment.* FRANK *gives* ROB *a model boat he has carved.* AUNT MARY *hands* ROB *a rose.*

ROB: I love the smell of roses. Why aren't these kind of roses anywhere else?
MARGARET: Because they're old-fashioned roses. I suppose people just stopped growing them.
ROB: Huh. People!

He goes to where the lily pool should be, confused.

Aunt Mary, what's happened to the lily pool?
AUNT MARY: It's been filled in.
SUSAN: To protect the children.
MARGARET: One of you children might fall in and drown.
ROB: Children. Huh!

He examines Chinese calligraphy on the wall.

What's that, Aunt Mary?
AUNT MARY: That? That's Chinese writing.

ROB: Who wrote that?

AUNT MARY: The Chinamen who built the house. I don't suppose anyone noticed them doing it.

ROB: What does it mean?

AUNT MARY: I've no idea. We hope it means: 'Good luck to this house', or something like that.

ROB: That's nice. Good luck to this house… Funny if it means: 'The Maplesteads are mad'! [*He takes a drink from a water bag.*] I like the water here—rainwater. It tastes like itself.

AUNT MARY: Oh look, twenty-eights in the olive trees.

ROB: Green fire. I'm very happy here, Aunt Mary.

AUNT MARY: Then you must be happy if you know it.

ROB: Because I know it now? Not later on?

AUNT MARY: Usually one knows afterwards, long afterwards.

ROB: Will the war be happy, afterwards?

AUNT MARY: Perhaps, for some people. Some people's memories are always happy.

ROB: My memories are always happy.

SCENE TWELVE

THE HAND CAVE

The group begins to travel. DIDI *is wearing a horse harness.*

NAN: Where does Daddy live?

MARGARET: I told you, he lives in the garrison.

NAN: With Uncle Rick and Edgar?

MARGARET: No. Uncle Rick and Edgar are winning the war.

ROB: It's a whole year since Rick went away.

NAN: Uncle Rick's dead. Uncle Rick and Uncle Edgar got killed in the war.

ROB: They did not! The Japs are keeping them!

NAN: Then they'll torture them.

MARGARET: Nan! Rob! Please.

The kids scatter. MARGARET *turns to* AUNT MARY.

AUNT MARY: They won't remember long.

MARGARET: It wouldn't be so bad if only the children didn't have such a thrill on Rick.

They approach an abandoned homestead.

ROB: Gosh—whose house is that?

AUNT KAY: Nobody's, it's abandoned.

ROB: Look at those palms.

MARGARET: Aren't they tall! Look at the garden, it's a jungle.

NAN: I'm a tiger.

She growls.

DIDI: I'm a horse.

DIDI *neighs and lunges in her harness.*

ROB: You're strong. Stronger than a boy.

DIDI: I don't want to be a boy. I want to be a horse.

DIDI *canters into the house followed by* NAN.

AUNT MARY: Mmm… smell the citrus and eucalyptus.

AUNT KAY: We used to go to dances here a long time ago.

ROB: Is it an ancient ruin, Mum?

MARGARET: Well, no. It's Edwardian.

AUNT KAY: This was the ballroom. All gone now, all ruined…

NAN *and* DIDI *open a door to another room.*

NAN: Look, a room full of tricycles.

ROB *looks up at a window in the house, then freezes. He has seen a ghost.*

Rob, do you want a ride?

ROB: No… I'm going upstairs.

MARGARET: No, Rob. You might fall through the staircase.

ROB: Well, why is that man allowed to, then?

MARGARET: What man?

AUNT KAY: Yes, what man, Rob?

ROB: The man at the window upstairs. I saw him.

ROB *runs outside followed by the group.*

AUNT MARY: Where?

ROB: Oh, he's gone. [*Excited*] Aunt Kay! I saw a ghost!

The group continue their walk towards the Hand Cave.

AUNT KAY: Well, perhaps you have the second sight like our grandmother.

AUNT MARY: I sometimes feel like I have the second sight. After all, our grandmother had it, and I am the seventh child of a seventh child.

MARGARET: [*to* SUSAN] Listen to the weird sisters!

AUNT KAY: You girls don't believe in anything.

ROB: Mummy believes in something. She thinks she's a water-diviner.

MARGARET: So I am.

AUNT MARY: And there's no question about that. We all saw you divine a forty-foot well with a windmill on it.

NAN: Where are we going. When will we be there?

MARGARET: We're going to the Hand Cave.

ROB: What's the Hand Cave?

MARGARET: Just you wait and see.

They approach the cave and stand in awe.

Look, Rob, at the old blackfellows' hands.

ROB: Hands. Whose hands?

NAN: Are they dead?

AUNT KAY: Oh, long ago.

AUNT MARY: It's a pity Ernest has such a down on the blackfellows.

AUNT KAY: I used to think the Sandalwood stockmen were so colourful, with their bright shirts.

AUNT MARY: Poor creatures.

NAN: Are they like the blackniggers in town? Did the blackniggers in town make the hands?

MARGARET: No, quite, quite different. These ones lived in the Old Days.

ROB: What's wrong with the blackniggers?

MARGARET: Oh, nothing. They've got bugs in their hair, that's all.

ROB: How did they do it, Aunt Kay?

AUNT KAY: They put their hands on the wall and filled their mouths up with clay and water and then went *prrumph* like a horse, and sprayed it all over their hands and left the marks on the wall.

ROB: Gosh!

ROB *discovers a handprint the same size as his own.*

AUNT MARY: Look, it's a little boy's hand.

CHORUS: He felt the cold rock under his hand where a dead boy's hand once rested. Time and change had removed the boy from his country, and his world was not one world but had in it the camps of the dispossessed. Above the one monument to the dead black people, the wind in the she-oaks sounded cold, colder than rock.

The group dissolves as the children pick up billies and knives and begin to hunt for mushrooms.

♦♦♦♦♦

SCENE THIRTEEN

AMNESIA

CHORUS: The first May rain fell again. The hard, sharp land of Sandalwood grew soft under green, and the disc plough sliced up the fallow. Armed with billies and table-knives the children went to the paddocks to hunt for new white mushrooms.

ROB: Over there… under the tree.

DIDI *steps in a cowpat.*

DIDI: Oh, shit!

NAN: Ummm ahhh.

ROB: You shouldn't say that.

DIDI: Why shouldn't I?

ROB: It's a dirty word.

DIDI: It's not a dirty word.

ROB: It is. I know it is.

DIDI: What does it mean, well?

NAN: It doesn't mean anything, it's just a dirty word.

DIDI: It's not a dirty word. Do you think I wouldn't know if it was a dirty word?

ROB: I give up.

Fed up with the other kids, ROB *moves away and climbs a tree.*

NAN: Don't, Rob. Mum said.

ROB: I can if I want to.

NAN: Umm ahh. I'm telling Mum.
ROB: Oh, shut up.
MARGARET: [*calling*] Rob!
ROB: I'm the king of the castle, and you're the dirty rascal!
MARGARET: Rob, where are you? Nan! Where's your brother?
NAN: He's up the tree.
MARGARET: Rob Coram, you come down this minute!
ROB: [*surprised*] I can see everything. Green, green and burning.

ROB *falls from the tree. Bright sunlight fades to black. He is carried to his bed.*

RICK *appears through the door, only his face lit. He moves towards* ROB.

Rick, Rick, you look funny. You've got three noses. Rick, why is it still night-time? Rick... Rick...

RICK *vanishes, to be replaced by* NAN *and* MARGARET.

Nan... Mummy, Mummy...

AUNT KAY*'s face appears and the light builds as* ROB *regains consciousness.*

Am I—am I sick? My voice sounds funny.

The rest of the family is now around him.

FRANK: He won't last the night.
ROB: Where's Rick? Rick was here. He looked funny. Where is he?
MARGARET: He wasn't here, darling, you were dreaming.
ROB: I saw him. [*He starts to cry.*] I want Rick. Please. Where's Rick? What happened?
AUNT KAY: You were dreaming, Robbie. You were delirious, don't you remember?
ROB: I want Rick.
NAN: You fell from a tree. There's a big hole where you hit the ground. You nearly died.

ROB *slowly rises to his feet during the following.*

CHORUS: He had walked into the darkness of amnesia, spreading out like a stain from the moment of his fall. Time, therefore, was more mysterious than he had guessed. Time confused him and possessed his mind, like a riddle which might have the answer to every riddle.

The group and ROB *inspect the site of the accident.*

ROB: Is that where I had the accident, Mummy?

MARGARET: Maybe.

ROB: Are we looking for something?

MARGARET: Yes, darling, you could say that.

ROB: Are we looking for my memory?

MARGARET: Perhaps it's that tree, with the big hole where you hit the ground.

ROB: I don't remember, I just don't. Mummy, did I really dream Rick? Wasn't he there?

MARGARET: You know he's away, darling.

ROB: I was sure he was there. I think he was, really…

MARGARET: Rob—

ROB: Yes?

MARGARET: Please don't talk about Rick. Not here.

ROB: Why? Why?

MARGARET: It upsets Aunt Mary. Just forget him.

ROB: I can't. I can't forget Rick.

MARGARET: Well, don't talk about him, except to me.

ROB: Did Rick get killed in the war?

MARGARET: No! Well—we don't know.

ROB: If he got killed, someone would tell you.

MARGARET: Not—where Rick is, in Malaya. He might be a prisoner. The Japs might be keeping him—

ROB: They'll torture him.

MARGARET: Rob! Don't talk like that.

ROB: I want Rick home. I want him home.

It starts to rain.

MARGARET: It's starting to rain. Let's find some cover.

They run through the rain and find shelter.

ROB: Can I write to Rick?

MARGARET: Yes, yes, we can keep sending letters, and hope he gets them. Aunt Mary and Susan do.

ROB: If I think to him, he might hear me thinking.

MARGARET: Yes, think to him, that's what all the rest of us are doing. And perhaps, when you thought you saw him—

ROB: I know. I know he was thinking back.

MARGARET: We'll start when we go back to Geraldton.

ROB: Are we evacuating again?

MARGARET: Yes. We're going back home, now that you're feeling better.

ROB: But this is home...

MARGARET: We need to give Aunt Mary a rest from us. We've been here three months and you've been quite a worry.

ROB: [*proudly*] Yes. Mummy, if I think to Rick, he might hear me thinking.

MARGARET: Yes, think to him. That's what all the rest of us are doing. And perhaps, [*confidentially*] when you think you see him—

ROB: I know. I know, he'll be thinking back.

MARGARET *takes* ROB *by the hand and prepares to run.*

MARGARET: Rob, quickly. Or we'll get soaked.

ROB: Goodbye, Sandalwood.

♦♦♦♦♦

SCENE FOURTEEN

THE RAILWAY

It's still raining on the railway. RICK *enters.*

RICK: How're you feeling, fella?

HUGH: I'm feeling pretty good, but I ain't felt nothing today. Rick...

RICK: Yeah.

HUGH: Rick—I drank your water.

RICK: That's all right.

HUGH: No, no—bastard of a thing to do.

RICK: Don't be stupid. What's a mate for? Edgar died. I just put him on the fire.

HUGH: He was family, wasn't he?

RICK: Yeah. He was so light, so dry. He burnt like twigs.

HUGH: Rick?

RICK: Yeah.

HUGH: I think I'm gunna die, mate.

RICK: No you're not.

HUGH: I reckon I've had it, Rick.

RICK: You're not going to die. In a pig's arse you're going to die. Get hold of yourself.

CHORUS: There's a long, long trail a-winding
To the land of my dreams...

RICK: We're young, Hughie, we're young. We're young...

The CHORUS *continues with the song as light comes up on* ROB.

ROB: Dear Rick,

I hope you will be home soon. I am seven years, ten months and four days old, and weigh four stone, six pounds, four ounces. I have been sleeping often in your room and have used your hairbrushes. I hope you don't mind.

Love from Rob.

SCENE FIFTEEN

TOWN

A noisy pub, full of servicemen, erupts into life.

REG: Hey, you!

ROB: What?

REG: Don't just stand there, come an' have a drink!

ROB: I'm not allowed to. Thank you very much.

REG: Watcha doin'?

ROB: I'm waiting for my mother.

REG: Where d'yerz live? You a bush kid? I'm a bush kid.

ROB: You're not very old, are you?

REG: I'm eighteen. Eighteen and never been pissed.

Another man appears in the doorway.

TOM: Save it, will ya?

REG: I got a mate. 'E's a bush kid like me, an' 'e never let a drop past 'is lips. [*To* ROB] Washa name, kid?

ROB: Rob.

REG: My name's Reg, an' tha's' Tom, the deadliest murphy peeler in the forces.

ROB: How do you do?

TOM *nods and then heads back to the bar.*

REG: Watcha doin' 'ere, kid?

ROB: Just waiting for my mother.

REG: Whyn'tcha go an' buy yerself an ice-cream or somethin'?

ROB: I haven't got any money.

REG: 'E 'asn't got any money. [*To the blokes*] The poor kid 'asn't any money!

TOM *appears.*

TOM: [*tossing a coin*] Here, kid—catch!

TOM *goes back inside.*

ROB: Gosh—sixpence! Thanks!

REG: [*louder*] 'E 'asn't got any money, the poor kid 'asn't got any money!

More money comes flying out from the doorway.

The poor kid 'asn't got any money!

ROB: I've got lots of money!

REG: You've got enough for an ice-cream, kid?

ROB: [*counting*] Gosh! One and nine-pence ha'penny—I've never had this much money.

REG: I'll tell you somethin', kid, just for yer own good. Don't spend it on women.

ROB: No.

TOM: [*from the bar*] Hey, Reg! Ya gunna let me drink this?

REG: I'll see yer, kid.

REG *disappears into the pub.* ROB *looks down at the pennies he's holding in both hands.*

ROB: Gosh.

MARGARET *enters.*

MARGARET: Where are you going? I told you to stay in the car.

ROB: I was going to go shopping. I was going to Snells to buy some presents for the soldiers.

MARGARET: What with? Why?

ROB: [*showing the money*] They threw me all this, so I was going to buy them something.

MARGARET: That won't buy many presents for a bar full of soldiers.

ROB: Well, something. Ice-creams or something.

MARGARET: [*giggling*] I'd almost give a donation, just to see a line-up of soldiers licking ice-creams at the bar.

ROB: Well?

MARGARET: No, Rob, they don't want anything. They've got plenty of money to throw away.

She starts to march off.

ROB: But it's for Rick.

His mother doesn't hear him.

♦♦♦♦♦

SCENE SIXTEEN

SCHOOL

A mêlée of schoolyard games. The girls skip to 'salt, mustard, pepper'. Boys play 'branders' and marbles.

KEVIN: Hey, youse kids gunna play branders?

ROB: Yeah. Who's got the ball?

GRAHAM: Here.

KEVIN: It's like the war, Graham's the Jap.

ROB: If it was the war, Graham wouldn't be the only one with a grenade.

GRAHAM *brands* KEVIN.

KEVIN: Aw, gawd, what was that? A mortar?

The school bell rings and the kids assemble in the classroom.

KEVIN *stumbles through the famous stanza from Laurence Binyon's poem 'For the Fallen'.*

They shall not grow old, as we that are left grow old;
Age shall not weary them, nor the years condemn;
At the going down of the sun, we shall remember them.

Lights come up on the rest of the classroom.

TEACHER: I don't think you've learnt that very well, Kevin... Now... Rob.

ROB: I like this poem because it reminds me of my cousin Rick Maplestead.

Our Andy's gone with cattle
'Gainst the drought, the red marauder.
Our Andy's gone with cattle now
'Gainst the Queensland border.
He's left us in dejection now
Our hearts with him are roving.
It's dull on this selection now
Since Andy went a-droving.
The gates are out of order now
In storms the 'riders' rattle.
For far across the border now
Our Andy's gone with cattle.
Oh, may the showers in torrents fall
And all the tank run over;
And may the grass grow green and tall
In pathways of the drover;
And may the good angels send the rain
On desert stretches sandy;
And when the summer comes again
God grant us 'twill bring Andy.

TEACHER: [*deeply moved but trying to hide it*] You've learned the words, but try to say them with some expression, Rob.

The students whisper to each other.

GRAHAM: Gee, it's hot.

KEVIN: I reckon it's a hundred and ten.

ROB: It was a hundred and seven at lunchtime.

The school bell rings.

TEACHER: Because the temperature is over a hundred, the headmaster has decided that school will finish now.

KEVIN: But it's only two-thirty.

TEACHER: Boys and girls who have to go on the school bus are to meet Miss Jones outside the boys' shed and she will take them for a swim.

Giggles from the boys.

Class, stand. Girls first, then boys.

The bell rings again and the class disperses.

GRAHAM: You going to the beach?

ROB: I'm not allowed to go by myself. Are you?

GRAHAM: Nuh. Not till I learn to swim.

ROB: We could go with the bus kids.

KEVIN: We've still got to go home to get our bathers.

ROB: D'you remember when we were little kids, that merry-go-round near the jetty?

GRAHAM: Yeah, and what about that merry-go-round your dad built for ya. Gee, he's clever.

ROB: Yeah, he made it out of a windmill.

GRAHAM: Yeah. I was mad on that.

KEVIN: Ah, it's for little kids—Hey, look! It's the micks from Stella Maris.

The boys jump up and down, slinging off.

BOYS: Convent dogs
Jump like frogs
In and out of water.

ROB: Ouch! I got a double-gee.

ROB *removes it and steps onto the bitumen.*

KEVIN: The tar's melting.

ROB: It's burning my feet off… Hoo, crikey!

GRAHAM *finds some shade.*

GRAHAM: Come over here, you drongos.

ROB: Jiminy, that burns. Hey, that'd be a good way to torture someone.

KEVIN: I reckon the best way to torture someone would be to make 'em drink petrol and then drop a match down 'em.

ROB: Aw, the match'd go out.

KEVIN: No it wouldn't. They'd be breathing all those fumes.

GRAHAM: What do you want to torture people for?

KEVIN: Aw, I don't know really. Be interesting, though, wouldn't it, to have a Jap to mess around with?

ROB: D'you ever get a date palm thorn stuck in you? That'd be a good way to torture someone.

KEVIN: No prize for second. The Japs have been doing that for years.

GRAHAM: How'd you like to be tortured? How'd you like to have all your fingernails pulled out?

ROB: I'd hate it.

GRAHAM: Why don't you shut up about it, well.

KEVIN: Don't get off your bike. No harm in talking.

GRAHAM: I bet you wouldn't think so, if your brother was in Bougainville.

ROB: Aw, cut it out. It was just a game. You don't have to bring real people into it.

KEVIN: We might just as well wear sandals, I'm not gonna have any feet left when I get home.

GRAHAM: Softy!

KEVIN: No nigger blood in me, I got white man's feet.

GRAHAM: [*threateningly*] Yeah? Who d'you reckon's got nigger blood here?

KEVIN: I bet Rob's got nigger blood. He's got a nigger mouth.

ROB: Yeah? You say that again.

KEVIN: All right. You got a nigger mouth.

ROB *pushes* KEVIN. *They dance a few steps on the hot tarmac, then jump back into the shade.*

Hey, you reckon they're black all over?

ROB: How'd I know? I never had a bath with a nigger.

KEVIN: Garn, I bet your old man's a nigger. Didn't you ever see him in the shower?

ROB: You shut up, my old man's a soldier.

KEVIN: All right. He can be a nigger soldier, can't he?

GRAHAM: They reckon they're good soldiers, some of the noogs.

KEVIN: I bet Keith Johnson'd be a good soldier, gee he's a tough kid.

ROB: I don't reckon he'd get into the army. He's thirteen and he's only Third Standard.

GRAHAM: Well, he hardly ever comes to school. They have a good life, these noogs.

KEVIN: I know what he does all day. He's up in the sandhills rooting the girls.

ROB: Gee, I don't know… I wonder what they get out of it.

KEVIN: Aw, they're just stupid. Makes me sick hearing big kids giggling like tarts.

GRAHAM: They don't do anything. They just talk about it.

KEVIN: Hey, did youse hear about Miss Jones?

GRAHAM: What about her?

KEVIN: Brian Carter saw her doing it with a soldier in the sandhills.

ROB: Aw, go home. You think we believe that?

KEVIN: It's dinkum. Honest. Brian saw it.

GRAHAM: Why don't you shut up, you dirty cow.

KEVIN: Yeah?

GRAHAM: Yeah.

KEVIN: Yeah?

GRAHAM: Yeah!

KEVIN: [*overlapping*] Old Val's going to have a baby.

ROB: What's she want to have a baby for?

KEVIN: Aww—old Jack's been rooting her.

ROB: Ah, what's that got to do with it?

KEVIN *and* GRAHAM *look at him.*

KEVIN: You can't have a baby without that. You know? Like taking a cow to a bull.

ROB: No… They're made in a sausage factory.

GRAHAM: [*sniggering*] Yeah, by the government!

ROB: Yeah, geez Kevin, you're a drongo! Hey, I'm gunna be eight next week.

KEVIN: Huh, Grandpa. You having a party?

ROB: I dunno. Parties are kids' stuff.

GRAHAM: I reckon if you go to some little kid's party you have a better time than if you have a party of your own.

ROB: You don't get presents, but.

GRAHAM: If you have a party, you never get anything except books and snotrags anyway.

ROB: I had some beaut parties before the war.

KEVIN: You don't remember before the war.

ROB: I do. Before the Jap war.

KEVIN: You don't remember before Hitler.

ROB: I bet I remember more than you do.

A SCHOOLGIRL *runs on.*

GIRL: Hey, youse boys!

BOYS: What?

GIRL: The Dings have surrendered!

ROB: Aw, they're always surrendering.

GIRL: No, this is dinkum. They've signed a treaty or something.

GRAHAM: Gee, maybe the Dings will fight the Jerries now.

GIRL: That's what they reckon.

KEVIN: Gee, I dunno, funny if it was the end of the war.

ROB *enters Grandma's house. The family are having afternoon tea.*

ROB: Did you hear? Italy's surrendered.

AUNT KAY: Good enough for them.

ROB: Yeah.

MARGARET: Rob—don't say 'yeah', or 'gunna', or 'ay', or 'shut up'. You are beginning to talk like a state-school kid… I mean child.

ROB: Of course I talk like a state-school kid. I'm going to the state-school, aren't I?

MARGARET: And don't contradict.

ROB: Nuh, I mean no.

He inspects the sandwiches on offer.

Ergh. Cold mutton.

MARGARET: Rob!

ROB: Aw, all right.

He takes one.

Grandma, have I got any nigger blood?

GRANDMA: Of course not!

ROB: Have I got any convict blood?

GRANDMA: Certainly not!

ROB: If I had convict blood and nigger blood, I'd be related to just about everyone in Australia.

AUNT KAY: No, you wouldn't be related to any Italian fishermen, or any Greek tomato-gardeners.

GRANDMA: Or any bog-Irish Catholics.

ROB: Uncle Ernest's a Catholic.

MARGARET: That's quite different.

ROB: What about Salvatore the eyetie POW? He reckons he can go home now the allies are in France.

He goes to grab another sandwich. MARGARET *stops him.*

MARGARET: Don't spoil your dinner. Aunt Kay is making us kedgeree.

ROB: What's that?

AUNT KAY: It's made with rice.

ROB: Rice? We haven't had rice for ages. Not since before the war. Do you reckon Rick gets plenty of rice in Malaya?

AUNT KAY: I expect so.

ROB *smiles.*

MARGARET: What are you laughing at?

ROB: I'm thinking to Rick.

A vision of RICK *and* HUGH *in the jungle. They are eating rice.* ROB *laughs,* RICK *and* HUGH *return the laughter.*

Oh, come home. Come home, Rick, and Edgar too. The Dings have surrendered, and it's going to be peace.

♦♦♦♦♦

SCENE SEVENTEEN

SUSAN'S LOSS

At the tank, ROB, KEVIN *and* GRAHAM *are set up for Chinese water torture with a large pannikin. On the other side of the stage a* MAN *approaches* SUSAN. *Everything stops.*

MAN: I suppose you know who I am?

SUSAN: Yes. And I suppose you know who I am.

MAN: Yeah, you'd be Mrs Bradley, wouldn't you?

SUSAN: I know you didn't really want to talk to me. But I did want to know. Won't you take a seat? This must be awful for you.

MAN: No, no, I don't mind talking about it. It's just that—I didn't know how you'd take it, I thought you might be—you know?

SUSAN: That was over long ago.

MAN: Yeah. Yeah, it would be.

SUSAN: But you, are you quite well now?

MAN: Ah, I'm fit, I feel good.

SUSAN: It must be like a dream, to be home.

MAN: It was a dream all right, at first. But now the other thing seems like a dream.

SUSAN: You were lucky.

MAN: You didn't need to tell me. When we got on that ship, I was dead sure I was going to die in Nippon. And when we got hit, all I could think of was that I was gunna die in the water. Then suddenly no more Nips, back to Mum and home cooking. That was luck, all right.

SUSAN: I've heard that you knew something about my husband, Edgar. It's all right, I'm not going to be emotional. It's just that I heard—I heard that you'd said Edgar died in Thailand, and I wanted to—hear it from you. It's true, isn't it?

MAN: Yeah. He—he died quite easy, you know, and—Rick Maplestead looked after him real good, he couldn't have had a better mate than that. I wouldn't worry about him now, 'cause—well, compared to things that might have happened, what happened to your husband was—real easy, you know, real quiet. It couldn't have been better.

SUSAN: And Rick?

MAN: Rick was wearing pretty well up to just before I left. But then he was pretty crook. I dunno how that would have turned out.

SUSAN: Very sick?

MAN: You can't tell. I've seen soldiers—big strong blokes—just drop, and little blokes come through what oughter've killed them. You can't tell how things are gunna take people.

SUSAN: Do you think Rick's dead?

MAN: I dunno. Yeah. Yeah, I reckon he is. I'm not upsetting…

SUSAN: No. No, everything's fine. I wanted to know. Everything. You've been very patient and very kind.

MAN: If there's anything I can do—

SUSAN: Thank you, there's nothing…

KEVIN *gives* ROB *the pannikin.*

ROB: Here goes…

SUSAN: It was true. I knew it was… I feel so sticky now, I must go and wash my hands. It's like summer… [*She pours water on her wrists.*] There's nothing… I said goodbye… I said goodbye two years ago. Why this now, why this?

ROB, KEVIN *and* GRAHAM *begin the Chinese water torture. At the same time,* RICK *and* HUGH *are lying down in the jungle. Both scenes run simultaneously.* ROB *skols his drink.*

RICK & GRAHAM: [*simultaneously*] What's wrong with you?

ROB & HUGH: [*simultaneously*] I feel sick.

RICK: What have you been eating, you stupid bastard?

HUGH: A fella gave me a tin of powdered milk.

RICK: You lucky bastard, I've dreamt about powdered milk.

HUGH: It fills you up.

RICK: I dunno, here I've been, running around like a cut snake to get you some tucker, and you go and ruin your appetite.

HUGH: Gee sorry, Mum, what did you find?

RICK: You won't believe it. I got a pound of cheese.

HUGH: 'Struth.

KEVIN: I'm not gunna be able to chuck. Gee, why did we start this?

ROB: I dunno.

RICK: I've eaten half of it. You want the rest?

HUGH: No thanks. It's a rotten shame, isn't it, when food starts falling out of the sky and you don't enjoy it.

RICK: Once upon a time there was a couple called Mr and Mrs Vinegar who lived on cheese. I'm stuffed if I know how they did it. I bet they were constipated.

HUGH: Aaah, why does the conversation in this place always get around to shit?

RICK: 'Cause that's all a human being is here, just messed-up bowels.

HUGH: Shut up about bowels. The war's over. People don't have bowels in peace time.

KEVIN: Gee, we have some stupid ideas. I'm feeling crook... I'm going home.

RICK: Where are we going to live, Hughie?

HUGH: I dunno.

RICK: What are we going to do?

HUGH: Dunno.

RICK: Well, think of something quick—the war's over.

NAN *enters.*

NAN: Rob. Rob, you have to come home.

ROB: Why?

NAN: We're going to Sandalwood.

ROB: To see Rick?
NAN: I dunno. Mum just said you've got to come home.
ROB: See you, then.
KEVIN: Yeah. Thanks a lot for poisoning me.

KEVIN *exits.*

ROB *starts running as per arrival at Sandalwood, encircling* RICK *and* HUGH *in the jungle.*

HUGH: Rick?
NAN & DIDI: [*together*] Rob!
HUGH: Rick?
RICK: What?
HUGH: I'm going to chunder…

HUGH *exits.*

NAN: You're going the wrong way.
RICK: Lucky you, wish to Christ I could.

♦♦♦♦♦

SCENE EIGHTEEN

ROB GETS LOST

ROB: I'm not! Come on…
DIDI: You are so.
ROB: This is the quickest way back to Sandalwood.
DIDI: You'll get lost.
NAN: You'll get lost. We're not waiting for you. Rob! Rob!
ROB: I'll be home hours before you.

ROB *strides ahead, then hesitates and looks about as the stage revolve turns him around. He walks on, stops and the revolve reverses—this process repeats.* ROB *begins to panic. He speeds his step as it becomes darker and darker. He bumps into a barbed-wire fence, entangling his clothes and cutting himself. He frees himself and staggers on until he falls heavily.*

God! God!

He picks himself up and continues slowly. He stumbles over something. It is a sheep. Then he stumbles over another. He stops. It is apparent he is in a paddock full of sheep.

Sheep! Sheep!

He attempts to lie down next to a sheep but it runs away. Finally, he pulls himself up and continues on. In the distance, lights come his way.

Hey! Hey! Hey! You with the light!

It is MARGARET *and* AUNT MARY.

MARGARET: Rob Coram, where do you think you were going?

ROB: The short cut.

MARGARET: Some short cut.

ROB: I was all right. I was on my way home.

MARGARET: Nonsense, you're not all right. Get in the truck!

ROB: I am all right.

MARGARET: You stubborn, stupid boy. You could have frozen to death. Do you know how far you are from Sandalwood? What, are those tears?

ROB: I'm not crying! I could have died from darkness. You can, you know, you can die from darkness, and you don't cry.

MARGARET: Aunt Mary's brought back some good news.

ROB: About Rick?

MARGARET: Yes.

ROB: Is he coming home? When? Where is he?

AUNT MARY: He's in a camp, a sort of hospital. He's been eating and getting well.

ROB: When's he coming up here?

MARGARET: As soon as he's well enough.

AUNT MARY: He's coming up with one of his army mates, Hugh MacKay. He's such a funny boy. His father's a butcher.

ROB: Did you see him, Aunt Mary?

MARGARET: Rob.

ROB: Yes.

MARGARET: If Rick is—different—you mustn't say anything.

ROB: How different?

MARGARET: If he's very thin, or perhaps hasn't got all his teeth… or is just different.

ROB: No! He mustn't be different!

♦♦♦♦♦

SCENE NINETEEN

RICK'S RETURN

A figure appears. RICK *and* ROB *examine each other, as in a mirror.*

RICK: Hey, remember me?

ROB: [*whispering*] Yes. Rick.

RICK: You knew me. You hadn't forgotten.

ROB: You're—just the same.

RICK: Let's look at you. When I look at you, you remind me of me.

ROB: Yes, they reckon we both look like my grandfather.

RICK: You might say 'welcome home'. You might shake hands with your deadbeat cousin.

ROB: Aw, sorry. Welcome home.

RICK: So. How old are you these days?

ROB: Nine. Nearly ten.

RICK: Rising double figures. Well now.

ROB: I can ride, and swim, and play tennis.

RICK: You any good?

ROB: Nuh.

RICK: That's fine. I like to win.

ROB: Can I come and stay with you and sleep in your room?

RICK: You bet you can. And you can go on using my hairbrushes till you're as bald as a goanna.

ROB: Did you get that postcard? Gee, everyone said you wouldn't.

RICK: I got it, all right. It was the only mail I got in three and a half years.

ROB: Were you pleased?

RICK: I bawled.

ROB: [*doubtfully*] You bawled?

RICK: Yeah. Then I showed it to a fella called Hughie MacKay who didn't get any mail through all of the war, and he bawled too.

ROB: Gosh. I didn't mean it to be so sad.

RICK: So you weighed four stone, six pound, four ounces, and Hughie and I weighed five stone a piece.

ROB: Five stone. Gee, you must have looked funny.

RICK: You'd have got the giggles. Hey, do you still get the giggles?

ROB: Yeah.

RICK: So do I. Just being home makes me giggle. And all the people…

RICK *notices a pile of school books.*

How's school?

ROB: All right. It's just school.

RICK *picks up one of the books.*

RICK: What's this? Ah, an autograph book. So you've got to that stage.

ROB: It's got everyone in it. All the family, all the kids in my class, and the teacher.

RICK: Some of your little mates have got an earthy sense of humour.

ROB: Will you write in it?

RICK: What shall I write? Something really rude?

ROB: No. Something—something nice, like Aunt Kay.

RICK: Something homecoming? Right. [*He writes.*] First chance I've had to use this pen my old mum gave me. There's something really nice from *The Muses' Favourite Treasury of English Verse*, which I happen to know off by heart 'cause I had it when I was captured.

ROB: [*reading*] What does it mean?

RICK: I dunno. It's just poetry. You're the one who used to be keen on poetry.

ROB: Rick.

RICK: Got to go, mate. We've got to drink a glass of whiskey from the bottle Aunt Kay bought to celebrate the Relief of Mafeking.

ROB: I don't understand it…

Thy firmness makes my circle just,
And makes me end, where I begun.

Blackout.

END OF ACT ONE

ACT TWO

RICK HOME 1945–1949

SCENE ONE

RICK'S ROOM

Music. Night. RICK *and* ROB *are on their beds.*

CHORUS: War is a different country. It doesn't matter which side you were on, or if you won or lost, if you fought a war you became a citizen of another, extra nation not on the map.

RICK *rolls a cigarette. Just before he licks the paper, he thinks about something, gets up and goes to the mirror, pokes out his tongue and examines his reflection carefully.*

ROB: Do you think you're beautiful or something?

RICK: Yeah. Don't you?

ROB: Aw—you're pretty skinny.

RICK: I'll live forever. I really believe that.

ROB: [*laughing*] Say 'ah'.

RICK: You may laugh, but I think I'm a bloody marvel.

ROB: Rick?

RICK: Mmm—what?

ROB: Nothing. Just—I like being here.

RICK: You know something? So do I.

RICK*'s eyes have a dead look that* ROB *hates.*

ROB: Rick—don't look like that.

RICK: How was I looking?

ROB: Oh—sad.

RICK: Sorry.

RICK *finishes rolling another cigarette, which he lines up with about twelve others.*

ROB: Why do you make so many cigarettes every night?

RICK: I don't sleep too well. I'll probably smoke all of these.
ROB: That's bad for you.
RICK: Hey, Pollyanna, why don't you drop off?
ROB: You've got the lamp on.
RICK: Right. [*He blows it out.*] Now, die, will you?

RICK *gets into bed. Time passes.*

CHORUS: War has its own language and its own literature, its own art (caricatures and battlescapes) and its own music (brass bands, nostalgia, bawdy).

After a moment RICK *starts to cry. He sits up and lights a cigarette.*

ROB: Rick?
RICK: Mmm?
ROB: Are you all right?

He gets up and walks over to RICK *and comforts him, patting him on the head like a dog.*

Don't cry, Rick, don't cry.
RICK: [*grinning*] I'm not crying, matey. Well, I mean, when I was crying I was still asleep. *Tidak apa.*
ROB: What does that mean?
RICK: It means, 'Sport, we can't be worried'.
ROB: What were you dreaming about?
RICK: It doesn't matter, does it?
ROB: Was it sad?
RICK: Yeah, pretty sad.
ROB: Was it a nightmare?
RICK: Uh-huh. Sit down, Rob. I want to talk to you.

ROB *sits on Rick's bed.*

Now listen, fella, wouldn't you rather sleep somewhere else?
ROB: No.
RICK: You see, I have these dreams, and I yell out in my sleep, and that must wake you up. It must make you nervous, I reckon. Wouldn't you sleep better somewhere else?
ROB: No, I don't mind, honest. I just couldn't sleep somewhere else.
RICK: Well, you're a stubborn little offsider to have.
ROB: When you have bad dreams, I'll come and talk to you, like they

used to do to me, and then you'll forget about them.

RICK: Right. If I yell you'll come and wake me.

ROB: And I'll tell you a story or something.

RICK: Fair enough. Or just say, 'Don't cry, Rick', like you did then.

ROB: You thought I was funny, when I said that.

RICK: That's just it. I want to wake up laughing.

ROB: I never know when you're kidding. Why didn't you bring me back anything? Graham Maxwell's father brought him back a Jap skull and now all the kids are going to see it, and Graham thinks he's a hero or something. Why didn't you bring me back a Jap skull? You never brought me anything.

RICK: I wasn't a fucking soldier, I was a fucking slave.

ROB: [*cautiously*] Gee, you did get tortured, then.

RICK: [*with acid sarcasm*] You'd have been disappointed if I hadn't, wouldn't you?

ROB: [*flinching*] No. No, Rick.

RICK: Ah, go on. I bet none of your bloodthirsty little mates has got a cousin who was tortured.

ROB: Please, Rick, don't go crook at me.

CHORUS: When you have belonged to that country you do not really go back to known nations. You never lose your citizenship.

RICK: Come here, buster. You want to know the story, don't you? So you can tell the other kids.

ROB: No. No, I don't want to hear it now.

RICK: Well, I don't care about you, I want to tell it. [*He rolls up one of his pyjama pant legs.*] See my feet? It was a red-hot bayonet that made those scars. I was a bloody good thief, even that time they didn't have anything on me, they just hoped I might be what they were after.

ROB: How could they do that? How could you stand it?

RICK: Well, I had this happy knack of passing out cold if anyone laid a finger on me.

ROB: Agh.

RICK: [*losing interest*] Cheer up. It never was anything very spectacular.

ROB: Gee, that's really something to have to show people when you're old.

RICK: [*laughing*] Aren't you the slimy diplomat?

CHORUS: In that country everything dies and nothing breeds, but somehow it never ceases to exist, because while it is flourishing, its language and its songs become part of the experience of children, growing into heroic nostalgia, so that once every twenty years or so that nation is re-founded, and begins enthusiastically to die.

♦♦♦♦♦

SCENE TWO

TENNIS PARTY

Pong! The tennis party revolves on. JANE WEXFORD *plays* MARGARET. ROB *is keeping score, browsing through Rick's sketchbook.* HUGH *is chatting with* AUNT MARY, AUNT KAY *and the kids.*

KIDS: Stacks on the mill, more on still!
MARGARET: Children, leave Uncle Rick alone.
ROB: Game, set and match!

From left: Leonard Goulds as Rob Coram, Andrew Broadbent, Jess Mercer as Nan Coram and Kim Delury as Rick Maplestead in Black Swan Theatre Company's 2003 production. (Photo: Jurgen Lunsmann)

MARGARET: Thanks for the game, Jane.

JANE: I'm not much competition, Margaret.

ROB: I had a thrill on Jane Wexford. She had lovely brown hair and her eyes were the colour of sherry. Her legs were smooth and brown like a kid's back in summer.

JANE: Rob, do you want a game?

ROB: I'm not very good at tennis.

JANE: I'm not very good either.

ROB: If you're not very good you should play with Rick. He's good.

JANE: He's a terrible partner. If you miss a shot, he looks ready to murder you.

ROB: Aw, he doesn't mean it.

JANE: Anyway, Rick won't play again. He looks tired.

ROB: He's very lazy. He lies around all day.

JANE: Well, of course, he's not really well yet. He's still resting.

ROB: He looks all right.

JANE: Isn't he good-looking? I think he's terrific.

ROB: Aw, I dunno. He's not pretty or anything.

JANE: [*sighing*] He's marvellous.

ROB: Yeah, that's what he reckons.

RICK: All right. Who's next?

JANE: Not with you, you play for sheep stations!

ROB: Except Hughie.

RICK: I hate to lose. I even hate it when this kid beats me at draughts.

ROB: I only ever beat you once.

RICK: I won't forget it, I sulked for days.

JANE: I suppose that's natural after—Well, who does like to lose?

RICK: Natural, after losing the war? That what you meant, Jane?

JANE: I forget what I meant.

RICK: 'Cause you're right. I was on both sides, and both times my team lost.

ROB: [*feeling uneasy*] Are you and Jane going to play?

RICK: Come on, what are you waiting for?

JANE: No, I think I'll go up to the house for a little while.

ROB: [*feeling unsure*] Jane thinks you're good-looking. She says you're terrific.

RICK: Ah, the stupid bitch.

ROB: [*affronted*] She's not! Why do you swear so much?

RICK: Ah, habit. Matter of fact, when I first went into the army I promised myself I never would. These bloody camps, you know, they sound like a chook yard. All you can hear for miles around is NCO's going 'fahk, fahk, fahk'!

ROB: [*laughing to himself*] Fahk, fahk.

RICK: You dirty little bastard, shut up.

ROB: Why is Jane a stupid bitch?

RICK: Ah, the way she talks. [*As* JANE] 'How can you possibly justify the mass murder of all those innocent children?' And I say: 'Lady, if I had the use of the bomb there wouldn't be a city left standing in Nippon right now.'

ROB: [*uncertain*] Are you kidding?

RICK: No, I'm not kidding. I'd have wiped Japan off the map, and given them no choice to make a comeback against us. Because that's what the little yellow insects will do.

ROB: No, they're our friends now.

RICK: Balls.

ROB: If you feel like that why don't you talk to the War Crimes people?

RICK: What's the use? You can't cure a cast of mind.

ROB: Is this what you dream about?

RICK: Partly. Partly the present and partly the future…

ROB: No one else thinks like that.

RICK: [*indifferent*] I know. [*As* JANE] 'You know, you may not realise it, but you talk just like Hitler.' [*Losing interest*] Ah, forget it.

They look around at the tennis party. HUGH *and* AUNT MARY *laugh.*

ROB: Where's Hughie sleeping? Is he going to have my bed?

RICK: Now, look, you're not going to get jealous of Hughie, are you?

ROB: No. I just wondered.

RICK: We'll put a camp bed in the room for you. Hell, you could sleep a dozen blokes in a room that size and it'd still feel empty to Hughie and me.

ROB: All right. Good. You don't want me to go home?

RICK: Ah, no. You're the only person of my age I've got to play with.

ROB: [*happily*] I never know when you're kidding.

ROB *wanders over to where* HUGH *and* AUNT MARY *are talking.*

HUGH: I really did appreciate that, you getting out all those books on painting. I dunno, people nowadays don't seem to have that feeling for beauty that people had a while ago, when you can remember.

AUNT MARY: Yes, I do sometimes think that with all the roughness of life when we were young, there was a sort of fineness, too.

ROB: You oughta hear Hughie, gor'struth.

RICK: Why? Is he buttering up my mum again?

ROB: Is he ever.

RICK: [*with a snort*] Hypocrisy's Hughie's best sport. [*Within earshot of* HUGH] Pity they don't give cups for it.

ROB: He should be winning cups for tennis soon. He's beating you.

RICK: Isn't that the rottenest thing you've heard of? The bastard had hardly had a racquet in his hand till I offered to coach him. You'd think he'd have the decency to lose.

ROB: He's coming. He heard that.

HUGH: [*wandering over*] You bitching again?

RICK: Ah, go and sell someone a gold brick. I saw you charming the pants off my mum.

HUGH: She likes me. She knows I'm a soul. Hey, kid, what do you know about beauty?

ROB: Not much.

HUGH: Don't they teach you about beauty at school?

ROB: Nah. Only poems.

HUGH: So when are you going back?

ROB: I've got four weeks yet.

HUGH: It's not long, still you'll be with all your mates again.

ROB: I haven't got any mates now. I was too old for the class I was in, so they shoved me up one, and now I don't know anyone.

HUGH: What, your old mates reckon you're too good for them, do they?

ROB: Yeah, I s'pose so.

HUGH: [*to* RICK] Poor little bugger. It must feel like they made him a corporal.

ROB: My dad used to be a corporal. We've got an old broom stick in the shed that's got Corporal Coram carved on the handle.

HUGH: Gee, eh? What did he do with it, fly?

ROB: Uh?

RICK: Hughie doesn't like corporals. We didn't rise very far in the army.

HUGH: Ah, we just didn't have the initiative. We were just happy sitting at home knitting socks for Nippon.

ROB: Can you knit socks?

HUGH: You bet. Just give me a couple of sticks and an Imperial Japanese army pullover and I'll knit you a layette for your first baby.

ROB: [*laughing*] Aw. Where did you get the pullovers?

HUGH: Pinched 'em.

ROB: And you knitted them into socks?

RICK: That's right. And then we sold 'em to the Nips.

ROB: Aw.

RICK: You may laugh, but they thought very highly of our socks. Hey, mate—why don't we go into business? Something sort of, you know, masculine like Maplestead & MacKay—Hairy Socks for Phoney Englishmen.

RICK: He's off again, white-anting the Empire.

HUGH: No, I like the Poms. They've got a sense of beauty. I'm only stuffed if I know where they get it 'cause they all seem to live in rabbit warrens.

RICK: They sit in their rabbit warrens reading DH Lawrence. That's what does it.

HUGH: How disgusting. Where are all the balls?

ROB: In the blacks' camp.

HUGH: What?

ROB: That's what Aunt Mary calls Rick's room.

HUGH: [*to* RICK] You game to take me on, sport?

RICK: I don't play with you. You cheat.

HUGH: Well, I'm going to hit up against a wall, and I'm going to get so good that you're going to feel embarrassed about all those cups you bought yourself.

RICK: That was Joke Number 98A. Yak.

HUGH: Some day, you're going to feel lousy about the way you used to talk to me.

HUGH *exits to look for the balls.*

ROB *has returned to looking through Rick's sketchbook.*

RICK: Are you looking at my sketchbook?

ROB: Yeah, can I?

RICK: I don't know why you'd want to, it's a lorry-load of bulldust.

ROB: [*reading*] 'In that country everything dies and nothing breeds, but somehow it never ceases to exist.' Why did you write that instead of drawing?

RICK: Just to remind myself of what I wanted to draw.

ROB: It's like—This page's got blood on it.

RICK: Yeah, I know.

ROB: Whose blood?

RICK: Mine.

ROB: Gosh. What happened?

RICK: Well, my good friend Hughie MacKay and I were giving the Emperor a hand with a railway he was having trouble with, and one day while I was holding a spike and Hughie was holding a hammer, Hughie landed the hammer on my thumb. Which was a bit careless. But Hughie wasn't really interested in building railways.

ROB: Gee, I bet you swore.

RICK: I bet I did. I bet I would have booted him in the ring if he hadn't run.

ROB: [*looking at the book*] Errgh, this one is just a skeleton. Was he dead?

RICK: No, that's Hughie.

ROB: Ohh.

RICK: You're shocked?

ROB: Yeah. Yeah.

RICK: Perhaps you should be, while you're still young.

ROB: Did you look like that?

RICK: Most of the time. Except once when I had dropsy or something, and swelled up like a dead cow.

ROB: I've seen some awful things. For a while if you went to the pictures you always saw newsreels of the German concentration camps. But not—people you know.

RICK: You didn't believe those newsreels, did you? You didn't believe those people had ever been human?

ROB: No.

RICK: I wonder what you would've felt if you'd seen me in Singapore.

ROB: I dunno.

RICK: I think you'd have run away. I bet Jane, who thinks I'm so good-looking, would have run away. I think everyone would have run away except Hughie, of course; he's permanent.

ROB: We wouldn't have run away, but we would have felt different.

RICK: Mmm. Sick and sorry.

ROB: I s'pose so.

RICK: That's what's stupid. Because what's left when everything else is gone is what matters. And nobody knows what was left in Hughie and me except Hughie and me.

ROB: That's—that's lonely.

RICK: Yeah, it is. Because I've got a soul and I know it. Which is more than you can say, buster.

ROB: P'rhaps I'll get a soul, later on.

RICK: P'rhaps you will. Or p'rhaps, if you're lucky, you won't need one.

ROB: I'm going to see Hughie.

RICK: Be nice to him. Tell him he's big and beautiful and the stars say it's a good week for being elected president of the RSL.

ROB: Sometimes I think you're around the bend. Sometimes I reckon you don't know that you're talking, let alone what you're talking about.

RICK: If you'd just stop listening, I might be able to control myself.

ROB: Hell, it's not my fault.

RICK: 'Course it's your fault. How can I help pouring out my confidences when you're always waiting around like a gurgling drain.

ROB: Oh, ari-bloody-gato.

He exits.

♦♦♦♦♦

SCENE THREE

EMU HUNT

Emus come onstage, stop for a drink and look around. The revolve starts moving and ROB *appears on a horse behind them. They run away as* ROB *chases.*

ROB: Can't they go! Can't they just go! Yahoo! [*He dismounts.*] Ohh. That was terrific.

RICK *and* HUGH *enter.* HUGH *looks the worse for wear.*

RICK: Look at Hughie.

HUGH *is clutching his horse, his head buried in its mane.*

ROB: He was hopeless. He's scared of her.

RICK: Well, he's only a townie.

HUGH: You blokes made her nervous.

RICK: She hasn't got a nerve in her.

HUGH: She's a terribly high-spirited horse. She tried to gallop, or canter, or something.

RICK: So in return you tried to strangle her.

HUGH: I only wanted to stay on. It's you two bastards who put me on this animal. Now I'm going to be walking like Donald Duck for a week, and all because you feel inferior, 'cause you can't play tennis.

ROB: That was terrific, chasing emus.

HUGH: What do we want horses for when we can ride the emu?

ROB: Aww.

HUGH: No, listen. I'm being practical. Hell, think how long a horse is pregnant and then the colt's got to be broken-in after that. But emus, you'd just have to put a clutch of eggs in an incubator and you could have a whole fleet of 'em in a few weeks. You wouldn't even need saddles, with all those feathers. I dunno, I think it's shocking the way we waste our natural resources.

RICK: But how'd you feel about riding something that could turn its head and look you straight in the eye?

HUGH: What sort of man would you be, if you couldn't outstare an emu?

They all laugh.

RICK: I love this place.

HUGH: What I can't understand, is why you're not a farmer. Oh, excuse me, I mean grazier.

RICK: You know my feelings about manual labour. I'm never going to get my hands dirty again.

HUGH: But you were doing Law even before you joined up.

RICK: I dunno why exactly, I suppose I wanted to get away from the monotony of life, and just take from it what did me good. It still seems a fair enough arrangement—to be a holiday pastoralist, and work with your head for a living

HUGH: But why Law, for Christ sake?

RICK: Dunno. If you're brought up on the land and you want to do something else, it pretty well has to be one of the learned professions. I hardly even thought about it, I just did it.

ROB: [*to* RICK] Are you going to go back to uni?

RICK: Yeah. In March.

HUGH: I think you're nuts.

ROB: I think you're nuts too.

RICK: You could be right, but at least give me a few years to get sane again. Take old Frank, he seems to have everything he wants, just by not wanting anything.

HUGH: You're going to throw one of your dewy-eyed fits, so just remember that when you had nothing, you hated it.

RICK: Not all the time. Nor did you.

HUGH: Aw, let's go back, mate. Let's grab a boat back to Thailand. Jesus, didn't we have some good times there?

RICK: All right, all right. You don't have to bury me in sarcasm.

HUGH: I reckon I do. I reckon you're such a sentimental bloody maniac you're getting homesick for the Old School already.

RICK: That's it exactly. The Old School.

HUGH: Well, you matriculated, sport, whether you like it or not. And it's compulsory to grow up now.

RICK: I grew up and so did you. And we outgrew everyone. We lost our innocence. Only, you seem to have got yours back again.

HUGH: You ever heard about doing in Rome as the Romans do?

RICK: It's not doing, it's knowing. Un-knowing in the case of the Romans. Un-knowing what human beings are capable of. Un-knowing themselves.

HUGH: Un-know thyself. Yeah. Yeah, I like that. That's a good motto for any returning warrior.

ROB *yawns.*

We're boring the mascot.

ROB: Uh?

HUGH: I said we're boring you.

ROB: I wasn't listening, I was thinking, how could you use a bridle on an emu?

HUGH: Let's all consider this problem individually and we'll have a meeting on it tonight.

RICK *has stripped and started to wash himself.*

Hold it, Rick. I just want one more photo for the *Western Mail*.

RICK *gives the V for Victory sign in reverse.* HUGH *tastes the water from the tank and spits it out.*

If I was a sheep I wouldn't drink this. [*Taking his boots off*] Ah, this is beaut. How can you talk about sheep being 'manual labour'?

RICK: If you feel like that, sport, come back for shearing. I'll teach you if I can find a real maggot-ridden one for you to learn on.

HUGH: Ah, you hardened old veteran. You reckon you're tough just because you've had your hands on a bit of daggy wool.

RICK: Listen to him. He sounds like a Kimberley cowboy.

ROB: Gee, I'd like to go there, to the Kimberleys. They've got wild camels up there, and in the Northern Territory.

RICK: Ah, why don't we, eh, Hugh? Why don't we go to the Territory?

HUGH: Because I'm going to get a bloody job in a bloody shop in bloody Perth. So forget it.

RICK: Aw, Hughie. You're not going to work in a shop?

HUGH: Yeah, I am. I'm going to sell tennis racquets and golf balls.

RICK: I think you're nuts.

HUGH: I don't take risks, kid. Risks are for the birds.

ROB: A shop?

RICK: Gawd.

HUGH: [*to* ROB] You'll be able to start playing golf as well as tennis, and perhaps you'll get good at that too.

HUGH: Yeah, yeah. I'll learn to play all the rich buggers' sports and end up in high society.

RICK: A shop. That beats me.

ROB *strips off his shirt and starts washing.*

HUGH: You poor little drowned rat. Why don't they feed you?

ROB: Huh. Look who's talking.

HUGH: We should live forever. If I don't knock your block off for giving me lip. I do all right. But my regularity worries are over, thanks to his lousy cooking.

RICK: I can't get used to the way this delicate bugger complains. I've seen the day when you wouldn't turn down a nice steak of snake cooked by me.

ROB: Errgh!

HUGH: Hey, this kid's never tasted snake, or cat, or dog. How about we barbecue that useless dog of yours tonight?

ROB: No.

HUGH: You ever killed a sheep, kid?

ROB: No, but I've killed chooks, for Christmas and New Year. Mum held the legs and the chooks would look at me as their heads lay on the block. I hate killing things.

HUGH: I've killed sheep and calves. My old man taught me. He's a butcher.

ROB: D'you ever kill a man?

RICK: Let's get going.

HUGH: Who d'you reckon you are giving me orders? Anyone'd think you were the boss's son.

HUGH *moves off to his horse.*

ROB: [*to* RICK] What's wrong?

RICK: You like Hughie, don't you?

ROB: Yeah.

RICK: Well, don't say anything like that to him again.

ROB: I won't.

RICK: Maybe I can even tell you why.

ROB: Yeah, tell me. I won't tell anyone.

RICK: He feels bad because when he was first captured, before I met up with him, he let someone die. An Australian. A bastard of a man who went off his head in front of a firing squad, and said he loved the Emperor.

ROB: What happened? How did the man die?

RICK: Well, Hughie was pretty near dead himself, and he refused to carry this sod. And so the Nips shot him while he was lying on the ground complaining.

ROB: I don't know why he worries about that, I wouldn't.

HUGH *returns.*

This is beaut, isn't it Hughie?

HUGH: Sure is.

ROB: You glad you came up here?

HUGH: Couldn't be gladder. It couldn't be more like what I needed.

ROB: Why don't you stay?

HUGH: Well, I wouldn't mind it.

ROB: I wish you'd stay. I wish you were going to be here while Rick's away at uni.

HUGH: You're a nice little bugger, but it can't be done, sport.

RICK: How about seeing to those horses, Rob?

ROB: Aww. All right.

ROB *takes them offstage.*

RICK: [*to* HUGH] You really do want to? Still?

HUGH: Yeah, of course I do, you drongo.

RICK: It's not just this she-waited-all-through-the-war-for-me crap?

HUGH: You know bloody well there's nothing chivalrous about me.

RICK: Well, good on you. And good luck.

HUGH: Will you stand up for me, mate?

RICK: Be your best man, you mean? Yeah, of course.

HUGH: You're a good bloke.

RICK: Hell, it's no trouble. You're the one who's got to do all the hard work.

ROB: [*returning*] What are you talking about?

RICK: Hughie's going to get married, Rob, to a gorgeous blonde called Joy.

HUGH: She's not actually. She calls herself a brownette.

ROB: Oh. Oh. Good. What's she like?

HUGH: She plays hockey.

ROB: Oh. [*Quickly turning to* RICK] You won't get married, will you, Rick?

RICK: Not me. Risks are for the birds.

ROB: That's good. Oh, congratulations, Hughie.

♦♦♦♦♦

SCENE FOUR

FAREWELL

CHORUS: The sandy town shook with explosions as the piles of the first of the two rotting jetties to go were blasted from their bed. Huge grey timbers washed up on the surf beaches.

The town changed.

The empty, dirty-windowed shops were restored; the pokey, shabby shops grew yankee flash; the swinging doors came off the pubs; and the verandahs and wrought iron balconies over the main street were torn down, by order of the council.

MARGARET, AUNT MARY *and* GRANDMA *are sitting together.* ROB *notices that they are all looking through a box of mementos.* NAN *enters and they all start rummaging through photos.*

ROB: [*holding up a photograph*] Who's this?

MARGARET: It's an English jackaroo who used to work at Innisfail.

AUNT MARY: Poor lad.

GRANDMA: They said he was a very nice man.

AUNT MARY: He was shot by a native.

GRANDMA: A half-caste.

MARGARET: But nice.

GRANDMA: Yes, they said he was a very nice man.

AUNT MARY: He lived on his camp at Innisfail and Aunt Rosa was very kind to him.

GRANDMA: They were like Aunt Mary and Frank.

AUNT MARY *looks at* GRANDMA, *aghast.*

MARGARET: Then one day she went down to see him with the young English jackaroo.

GRANDMA: And just as they turned their horses to go…

AUNT MARY: Jacky picked up a gun and shot the jackaroo dead.

ROB: Gosh, why?

GRANDMA: I think he was just insanely jealous.

ROB: And what happened then?

GRANDMA: Well, he ran away into the bush, and they had a great manhunt. Everyone was terribly scared, of course.

ROB: And what about Jacky?

GRANDMA: They found him in the end, and he was quite, quite mad by then. They put him in the asylum at Claremont.

RICK *enters.*

ROB: Rick! Did you know there was this English jackaroo at Innisfail…?

RICK: You're just like Aunt Kay. Gaelic through and through. Just a fey old highlander.

ROB: Well, what's wrong with that?

RICK: Ah—violence is boring, fella. Boring. More boring than anything except peace.

ROB: Did you know that Great-Grandmother Maplestead hid Moondyne Joe under her bed?

RICK: You're not getting starry-eyed about poor silly old Moondyne Joe, are you?

ROB: Why not? He's the only bushranger we've ever had.

RICK: Some bushranger, bush-burglar's more like it. Just a housebreaker and horse thief who liked to hole up in a romantic cave in Great-Grandfather Maplestead's back paddocks

ROB: Well, if he wasn't a bushranger he was a sort of what-d'you-call-it, a Houdini. Heck, the governor built a special cell for him at Fremantle gaol and bet him he couldn't get out of it, and he got out with a spoon.

RICK: He was a pathetic nut, and he ended his career peddling aphrodisiacs.

ROB: What's aphrodisiacs?

RICK: Jane Wexford's an aphrodisiac.

ROB *goes to ask another question.*

No. No more questions!

♦♦♦♦♦

SCENE FIVE

LOVE ON THE BEACH

RICK *joins* JANE *on the revolving stage for a walk on the beach.*

CHORUS: The weed-strewn beach was sharply black-and-white in the moonlight, and the foam-lines in the shallows crawled like cream. Farther out, the black-and-white rollers folded over their hollows and shattered with an echoing boom.

JANE: The sea looks so dark and wild, how can fishermen bear to go out at night?

RICK: Are you cold?

JANE: I don't feel cold, but it looks cold.

RICK: Jane—

He puts his arm around her.

JANE: Don't be silly, Rick. I'm not cold, and if I was, one hairy arm wouldn't keep me warm.

RICK: Try two hairy arms.

JANE: Oh, stop it. It's not compulsory to act like this on the back beach.

RICK: I feel a compulsion. Jane, stop walking for a moment.

JANE *stops and turns to him.*

JANE: Why?

RICK: I want to look at you. You're beautiful, Jane.

JANE: That was a rather automatic remark.

RICK: Will you let me kiss you?

JANE: No.

He does.

Rick, I…

RICK: What?

JANE: I forget. I think I was going to say that you're not such a nice boy as everybody's mother thinks you are.

RICK: I only kissed you.

JANE: I'm not the village idiot, Rick.

RICK: What?

JANE: I don't like being taken out for a drive and then—vamped, or whatever the male version of vamping is. I suppose you and your friends have a revolting word for it.

RICK: I'm not that sort of lad. I'm much more like everybody's mother thinks I am.

JANE: And besides, I don't think I trust you. To care, I mean.

RICK: But I do.

JANE: I'm not even sure I like you. I don't see how I could like you, when I don't trust you. Though I do think you're very good-looking.

RICK: You're the only person who thinks so. That must mean something.

He goes to kiss her again.

JANE: Take me home, Rick.

RICK: Am I really as bad as all that?

JANE: No.

RICK: Just tell me one thing.

JANE: Well, ask.

RICK: What's wrong with me?

JANE: There's nothing wrong with you, and I love dancing with you, but this—this just makes me feel awkward.

RICK: Why?

JANE: Oh, because I think you want awfully much for someone to love you. And I don't want to. I don't think you'd love me back. I think you'd be very gentle and protective, and you probably would be, but I can't imagine you in love. I think you're—I don't know, frozen.

RICK: [*introspectively*] There's nothing there, that's what someone told me. There's nothing there.

JANE: Rick—what I've said doesn't mean that I don't care, I do want you to be happy.

RICK: And you'll follow my future career with deep interest?

JANE: Don't be sour with me. Just admit that you tried something that didn't work, and that we don't care much, and we'll laugh it off.

RICK: I think I really do make you nervous.

JANE: Yes. That's why I want to go back to the car.

RICK: Suppose I said that I loved you?

JANE: I wouldn't believe you.

RICK: Jane, you know what I want. Give it to me, for friendship's sake.

JANE: No, no, no, no. You're not my responsibility, and you've no right to tell me I ought to give you something that won't mean a thing to you tomorrow. I don't owe you anything, nobody owes you anything. Only babies can get things just by sounding hurt.

She walks on, leaving RICK *alone.*

RICK: There's nothing there, nothing there.

CHORUS: Her footprints, going away from him, made pits of darkness in the moonlit sand, and the black sea curled over its hollows with a hollow boom.

♦♦♦♦♦

SCENE SIX

BOYS' TALK

A racehorse goanna appears as ROB, KEVIN *and* GRAHAM *walk near the jetty.*

ROB: Graham, Kevin, look! A racehorse!

KEVIN: I wonder if I can hit him.

ROB: You fool, he'll come after us.

They climb a tree or windmill.

GRAHAM: I reckon we'd better climb farther up.

Trevor Jamieson as the goanna in Black Swan Theatre Company's 2003 production. (Photo: Jurgen Lunsmann)

ROB: That won't be any use. They can run up anything. They run up people and horses and down the other side.

KEVIN: Hell, I wish he'd nick off.

GRAHAM: It's no good trying to shoot through. They go like lightning.

ROB: Aren't you a clever bloody kid? I suppose we're going to spend the rest of our lives in this tree.

GRAHAM: Well, hell, they can't hurt you much. They only give a bit of a nip and then the sore comes back once every seven years or something. On the anniversary.

ROB: They can't have much strength in their jaws if they're anything like bobtails. We've got a goanna at home that comes every summer and I give it grapes, and its jaws are so weak it can hardly break the skin. Hey, you know something, it'll only drink out of a red cup. They like anything red.

KEVIN: You got anything red on you?

ROB: Yeah. [*Pulling out a red bandanna*] This.

KEVIN: Give us it. Now when I lob this near the old goanna we drop and run—get it?

ROB & GRAHAM: [*together*] Yeah.

> KEVIN *throws it on the goanna. The boys flee towards the revolve. They walk in silence for a moment.*

GRAHAM: Come to think of it—what are we scared of? Let's go back and kill it.

ROB: Ah no, we're always killing things.

GRAHAM: Well, what do you want to do?

KEVIN: Let's go to the end of the breakwater.

ALL: Yeah!

ROB: You see that stump thing sticking out of the water?

GRAHAM: Yeah.

ROB: Well, when I was a little kid the mast and the what-d'you-call-'ems were still there, and I used to think it was a merry-go-round. A merry-go-round in the sea.

KEVIN: That'd be good, a merry-go-round in the sea. You'd have to make it good and high, though, for diving.

ROB: I just thought of sitting on it, and dangling my feet in the water. I couldn't swim then.

GRAHAM: And you can't bloody well swim now.

ROB: How'd you like to go over the edge?

GRAHAM: Gee, I'm scared—listen to you. [*In a posh English accent*] 'Mrs Grahnt's got ahnts in her pahnts.'

ROB: Oh, listen to you. 'Mrs Graent went passt very plaent tomatoes.'

GRAHAM: Shall we dahnce?

ROB: Drop dead.

GRAHAM: You talk like a bloody Pommy.

ROB: I bloody well do not.

KEVIN: What are we going to do now?

ROB: You got your bathers on?

GRAHAM: Yeah.

KEVIN: Let's go swimming.

JANE WEXFORD *appears and sets up to sunbathe.* KEVIN *spots her.*

Hey, wait a minute!

ROB: What's up?

KEVIN: There's a girl over there.

GRAHAM: Ah, that girl there's Jane Wexford.

ROB: Well, she won't hurt you.

ROB *approaches and the other boys shyly follow.*

JANE: Hello, Rob.

ROB: Hello. Aren't you studying today?

JANE: No, I don't need to for a while. I've got a new job in Perth.

ROB: That's good. You'll be able to go around with Rick. Rick reckons you're an aphrodisiac.

JANE: [*laughing*] You horrible little boy!

She dives in for a swim. The boys move away.

KEVIN: What's an aphrodisiac?

ROB: I dunno, but Jane's one!

GRAHAM: You want to be careful what you say. It might mean a moll.

ROB: No. Rick wouldn't say that about Jane.

KEVIN: They reckon they saw a grey nurse in the harbour yesterday.

GRAHAM: They reckon there's a swordfish around, too.

ROB: Gee, I'd like to see that. Not while I'm swimming, but!

GRAHAM: [*picking something up*] Look what I found.

KEVIN: What is it?

GRAHAM: It's a girl's brooch with a blue bow on it.

KEVIN: Who're you going to give it to?

GRAHAM: Dunno. I might try and give it to Elizabeth, but I bet she won't take it.

ROB: Once I found a brooch with 'Mother' on it. Heck, you should have heard my mum when I gave it to her. You'd have thought it said 'Flossie' or something like that.

They approach the merry-go-round which has suffered damage over the years.

Hey, the merry-go-round.

KEVIN: The broken seats've been taken.

GRAHAM: Yeah, it's been wrecked.

ROB: I was mad about that when I was a little kid. Maybe when I'm grown up and rich I'll restore it. And I'll put a plate on it saying: 'Presented to the children of Geraldton by Sir Robert Corum Esquire'.

The brewery whistle sounds.

KEVIN: Hey, that's the brewery whistle.

GRAHAM: Five o'clock! Time for the *Argonauts*!

KEVIN: Race you home!

They leave ROB, *still lost in thought.*

ROB: … and I'd write on it that poetry Rick wrote in my book:

'Thy firmness makes my circle just,
And makes me end, where I begun.'

♦♦♦♦♦

SCENE SEVEN

ELLENBROOK

RICK *is trying to get a horse through the door. The sounds of kicking, and a bucket overturning as they enter the yards.*

RICK: Whooah.

The horse bucks out of the shed.

I don't think I like you, Ellenbrook. You look like a real prima donna.

The horse rears and continues to prop and pig-root.

But I think I can knock you into shape.

She rears again.

I don't think you like human beings, do you?

She snorts and trots about.

Proud too.

He circles the horse.

You know what you are? You're a narcissist. And aren't we a handsome couple?

She is settling now. Circling in a gentle manner.

What, are you listening, old girl? You're keeping track. You can hear the country you've left. It must be like music, growing fainter.

He slackens the rope slightly and she wheels around to go off in another direction—home. He reins her in again.

Come back, beautiful. Poor old girl. Memories can be a bloody nuisance.

She now hangs her head low and walks, simply moving her legs like an automaton.

Somebody's treated you badly, you poor hysterical bitch. But everything's going to be fine, so forget the bad things that happened, the past won't hurt you, and we can't be worried about the future. *Tidak apa.*

Ellenbrook, I know what it feels like, Ellenbrook, having to walk when you think you're done. I reckon I know what it feels like being you, Ellenbrook. But we can't all shy and rear at memories.

The CHORUS *sings the refrain 'Grievous Music' from Stow's poem 'Outrider'.*

The exchange between the music, actor and horse is abstract and dance-like.

CHORUS: My mare turns back her ears
And hears the land she leaves
As grievous music.

SINGER: My mare turns back her ears

And hears the land she leaves
As grievous music.

CHORUS: The year wore on. The merry-go-round of life revolved. In Asia there was a war, and in Perth the profoundest peace. The boy went back to school, to the high school now, and Rick went back to college.

♦♦♦♦♦

SCENE EIGHT

THE FLAT IN MOUNT STREET

RICK *and* JANE *lie on a rug on the sitting room floor of Jane's flat.*

CHORUS: It was autumn in Perth and in Jane's flat in Mount Street were vases of great bitter-smelling chrysanthemums. Jarrah blocks were burning brightly in the fireplace.

Kim Delury as Rick Maplestead and Ingrid Ruz as Jane Wexford in Black Swan Theatre Company's 1997 production. (Photo: Frances Andrijich)

JANE: I didn't want this to happen, I didn't.

RICK: Why not?

JANE: I don't know you.

RICK: But you do. You're my lover, Jane.

JANE: No, still, even now, I don't know you.

RICK: No one can know anyone better than this.

JANE: I wish it hadn't happened. Not here, not just now. Suppose Lucy's awake, she could have heard everything from the bedroom.

RICK: I don't care about Lucy. I love you, Jane, and Lucy's welcome to hear it.

JANE: Sshhh.

RICK: You're so scared and the back of your neck's so innocent. I won't let anything hurt you, not a thing.

JANE: Oh, Rick... I love you so much. I'm so frightened. Rick, be good to me.

RICK *mumbles something into* JANE*'s hair.*

Would you mind mumbling that again?

RICK: Will you marry me? Because I'm getting awfully sick of this hearth rug.

JANE: Oh, mate.

They kiss.

♦♦♦♦♦

SCENE NINE

THE ARTIST

ROB *looks out over the landscape as* RICK *joins him.* RICK *has brought his sketchbook.*

CHORUS: The folds of bare silver-brown land were marked with green wattle, and the farthest hills and the patches of cloud-shadow were dark sea-blue. Wattle suckers glowed malachite-green in the late light. The ewes climbed the slope to the yards and the randy rams came prancing to meet them. Light pierced the tawny dust in the air above them, and every head and horn and rounded rump wore a nimbus of furred silver.

RICK *is drawing.* ROB *looks over his shoulder at the picture.*

ROB: I dunno, everything you draw turns into prisoners of war.

RICK: It's my gimmick, like being a Catholic or a Commo.

ROB: Why don't you paint those sheep?

RICK: I might try, but it's too good really. It needs Turner.

ROB: Turner… Look at their green eyes, paint that, Rick!

RICK: I wouldn't have a hope. That's pre-Raphaelite stuff.

ROB: [*vaguely*] Oh, yeah.

RICK: You don't like my pictures, do you, mate?

ROB: Oh ye-es, but they're all the same. Do jungles really look like that… those colours?

RICK: Well, I'm only learning. I'm just a potterer.

ROB: I liked the self-portrait you did.

RICK: Yeah, even Mum liked that.

ROB: Yeah, but she said she could have guessed you'd paint a self-portrait.

RICK: Oh, yeah.

ROB: What makes you so sulky? Why won't you go anywhere people are?

RICK: Ah, I'm just a homebody at heart.

ROB: I dunno, you must be the laziest man in the world.

RICK: Yup. That's what keeps me young.

ROB: Don't get old, Rick.

RICK: I won't if I can help it. I don't think I could grow old gracefully.

ROB: Yeah, that's what makes you interesting.

RICK: What, my intolerence?

ROB: Yeah… [*Sending him up*] 'There's not a bloody leader in Australia.'

ROB & RICK: [*together*] Why can't we produce a Churchill or a de Gaulle?

ROB: [*goading*] Or a Hitler?

RICK: Well, Hitler had one or two qualities we could use. He wasn't a nonentity.

ROB: What's a nonentity?

RICK: Menzies… Casey… Fadden…

ROB: What you want's a hero. The sort of bloke I used to reckon a poet was when I was a little kid. Someone like Adam Lindsay Gordon.

RICK: But Gordon was a nonentity as a politician.

ROB: I know.

RICK: But he was the right kind of hero for Australia. Gloomy and romantic. And a good person to represent Australia in Westminster Abbey. He had a handsome head.

ROB: Lord Forrest was a hero. I don't suppose he would have been a politician at all if he hadn't been a hero first as an explorer.

RICK: Yeah. He doesn't excite me much.

ROB: Gee, I wonder if the J.F. on the Moreton Bay fig opposite the Geraldton Hotel really is John Forrest. Some of the kids reckon Johnny Field carved it there.

RICK: It probably was Johnny Field, then, whoever he is. The less interesting version's always the truth.

ROB: Who could be a hero? I don't know any heroes.

RICK: I reckon C.Y. O'Connor was a hero. A hero like one of the abos' heroes, the ones that went round the tribal country creating the animals and waterholes, and then vanished into the ground. He engineers this huge scheme to bring water to the goldfields and then just before it goes into operation he shoots himself. Vanishes into the ground. That was heroic.

ROB: They're all so sad, all the Australian heroes. They always die in the desert, or shoot themselves or something.

RICK: I reckon it's the Celt in us. I reckon you define Australia as an Anglo-Celtic vacuum in the South Seas.

ROB: Gee, you're rude about Australia.

RICK: I don't mean it. It's a good country to be a child in. It's a childish country.

ROB: If you think like that, why don't you go to England and live in a rabbit warren, like Hughie says?

RICK: Because, I'm engaged.

Jane's flat revolves in and RICK *steps up onto it.*

♦♦♦♦♦

SCENE TEN

THE FLAT IN MOUNT STREET

CHORUS: In Jane's flat, branches of cotoneaster stood in a large white jug, the berries brightly orange against the grey wall.

Vivaldi's 'Autumn' plays in the background.

RICK: This is good. Why don't we arrange for Lucy to be on night shift permanently?

JANE: I can't see that it would make that much difference. Lucy knows damn well what goes on.

RICK: Do you tell her about me? In intimate detail?

JANE: Don't be disgusting. As if a nurse would be interested anyway.

RICK: You're interested, aren't you?

JANE: I've never known anyone like you, for fishing for compliments. Would you like some coffee?

RICK: Oh, yes. I dunno. No. Stay here.

She leans against his shoulder.

JANE: Do you love me, Rick?

RICK: You don't really doubt that.

JANE: I do, sometimes. When you just sit, not talking, and looking grim.

RICK: It's the music. I can't help listening to it.

JANE: No, not always. I hate it when you sit like that. It makes me feel—boring.

RICK: Aw, Janie, you are a nit.

JANE: Why don't we get married?

RICK: Well, there's a little thing called money that newly-weds seem to set some store by.

JANE: We could if you wanted. Lots of ex-Service students are getting married.

RICK: I want it to be fun, not hard slogging labour. And I don't want you to go on nursing.

JANE: But I want to.

RICK: You'll do as you're bloody well told.

JANE: I don't know. I don't understand you. I don't think I ever will. So, let's have some coffee.

RICK: This is a nice flat. Shall we boot Lucy out and live here when we're married?

JANE: I bet Lucy's married herself, before then.

RICK: Don't be sour, honey.

JANE: Oh, stop it. Don't be charming to me.

RICK: You are having a lousy, aren't you?

JANE: Yes I am. And I give you fair warning, Rick Maplestead, if I get another proposal that doesn't mature like a savings bond, I'll bloody well take it!

RICK: Don't talk Eliza Doolittle to me.

JANE: Oh, Rick, you are annoying.

He kisses her on the neck.

RICK: Is this annoying you?

JANE: No.

RICK: Then shut up.

JANE: So much for the coffee.

Lights come up on:

♦♦♦♦♦

SCENE ELEVEN

TOWN LIFE

ROB, GRAHAM *and* KEVIN *sit with their backs to a wall enjoying the winter sun.*

ROB: What are we going to do? What the hell will we do when we grow up?

GRAHAM: I dunno.

ROB: I know what we ought to be. Farmers or fishermen.

KEVIN: I don't reckon we will be, though.

ROB: Everything we know that's got any sort of—dignity to it—is mixed up with the land or sea.

GRAHAM: But it's hard work, and we don't like hard work.

ROB: But there's something about, oh, mustering or getting the boat ready for the Abrolhos. Something that makes a man sort of fill up.

GRAHAM: Yeah. I'd reckon I was getting on in the world if I felt like they look.

LES, *a bigger, older boy, enters, accompanied by some other kids.*

KEVIN: Fight's on!

LES: I don't know, d'you ever see such a dirty-looking mob?

ROB: Hey, Les, which side are you going to be on?

LES: I ain't gunna be on no side. Whichever side I'm on, everyone else is on the other.

KEVIN: Beauty! Get him!

ROB: Pull his legs!

GRAHAM: Choke him off!

They all leap on him.

ROB: Give in?

LES: No.

KEVIN: Give in?

LES: Aw, all right.

ROB: Rub a lump of dirt in his face.

LES: All right! I give in.

ROB: Who's a dirty-looking mob now?

LES: You are. You're a dirty mob of fighters, too.

KEVIN: Here. [*He has a stinkweed in his grasp.*] Shove this in his mouth.

LES: All right. I'm a dirty-lookin' mob.

ROB: You're a dirty fighter too.

LES: An' a dirty fighter too. Takes one Chink to reckernise another.

KEVIN: When I count to three, I'm going to rub this in your face for calling me a Chink!

ALL: [*together*] One… two… three!

They scatter.

KEVIN: These big blokes haven't got the stamina.

ROB: I wonder what I'm going to be when I grow up.

KEVIN: Well, not a film star. And not an all-in wrestler.

GRAHAM: Why don't you be a drunk? You don't need any talents for that.

ROB: It's got to be something in your blood.

GRAHAM: That's a load of bulldust. Hell, Australia was built by people who didn't know who their grandparents were. You can be anything you want to be, and you ought to be what you want to be, not what your grandpa was.

ROB: [*demanding*] So, what are you going to be?

GRAHAM: A drunk! I haven't got any talents.

Lights come up on:

♦♦♦♦♦

SCENE TWELVE

THE FLAT IN MOUNT STREET

JANE: Sometimes I think I hate you.

RICK: What have I done now?

JANE: Do you know what time it is? Do you realise I've been waiting for two hours?

RICK: I'm sorry, I met Hughie.

JANE: I don't know why you didn't marry Hughie while you had the chance.

RICK: He didn't ask me.

JANE: Rick, I'm serious. I want to break this.

RICK: Janie, just because I'm late—

JANE: It's not that. You don't love me.

RICK: Jane—

JANE: And don't come near me. You reek of beer.

RICK: I'm a bit drunk.

JANE: A bit.

RICK: All right. I'm so drunk I couldn't scratch myself. I'm paralytic. But we're still engaged.

JANE: No. We're not.

RICK: I'll ring you in the morning.

JANE: I won't be in.

RICK: All right. I'll come in and wait on the doorstep.

JANE: If you come here I'll make you look like such a fool that you'll be glad to crawl home.

RICK: Okay. I'll get good and drunk before I come, and bring Hughie.

JANE: Oh, Rick—

RICK: Oh, Jane.

JANE: Go away and sleep it off like a good boy.

RICK: And we're still engaged?
JANE: I suppose so. Damn you.

SCENE THIRTEEN

A PICNIC OF DISAPPROVAL

The Maplestead clan and JANE *are gathered for a picnic.*

NAN: Uncle Rick, why aren't you married?
RICK: I'm going to get married, next year. To Jane, over there.
NAN: When?
RICK: Oh, I dunno. Ask Jane.
NAN: Can I be a bridesmaid?
RICK: You're a bit young. It's up to Jane to say.
ROB: Can I be best man?
RICK: What, in short pants?
ROB: Well, I'll be in long pants by then.
NAN: You'll look stupid.
ROB: You shut up.
RICK: Hey, I never talked to my sister like that.
ROB: I just heard you tell Susan to drop dead.
RICK: Ah, but she's grown-up now. She can take it.
ROB: [*to all the kids*] Hey, let's fight Rick!
RICK: No. No fair go!

They all leap on top of him.

I've never been so brutally treated in all my life. You must hate me.

ROB: They reckon that the funny thing about the Maplesteads is that they all like each other.

RICK: Well, God save me from demonstrations of affection from the Maplesteads.

JANE: I think togetherness is being carried a bit too far over there. Rick must be suffocating under all those children.

AUNT MARY: Isn't he good with children? It's odd, really, because he's not at all a patient man.

MARGARET: He's awfully nice, and he was an absolutely horrid little boy.

AUNT KAY: He was not! We were all very fond of Rick.

SUSAN: He was horrible. He was damnably spoilt.

AUNT MARY: Susan, I won't have you criticising the way I brought up my children.

AUNT KAY: I thought he was rather an interesting kid.

MARGARET: It's still impossible to see what he's going to be like when he grows up.

AUNT MARY: Yes. He's not really grown-up, although he's twenty-eight.

AUNT KAY: What do you think, Jane?

JANE: Oh, I don't mind. I don't want him middle-aged. And what does grown-up mean anyway.

SUSAN: Responsible. And he's not.

AUNT KAY: I think he's a good bloke.

MARGARET: I think he's a very likeable boy, in a rather conscious sort of way.

JANE: After this conversation, I think he's a cross between the Mona Lisa and the Sphinx. I wonder if anyone knows what he's like.

AUNT MARY: Oh yes, Hugh MacKay does. But I don't.

MARGARET: I think perhaps Rob does. He seems to be trying to turn himself into a carbon copy of Rick.

AUNT KAY: Poor wee lad. They are funny at that age.

SUSAN: Children! Leave Rick alone, and come and eat.

AUNT MARY *hands a plate to* JANE.

AUNT MARY: Will you take this to Rick?

JANE *moves over to* RICK.

RICK: Oh. food. Thanks.

JANE: Rick. Hadn't we better admit it, and call the whole thing off?

RICK *shrugs.*

RICK: All right.

JANE: Somehow, I knew you were ready for me to say that.

RICK: Things were running down. Perhaps we've found out all there is to know about each other.

JANE: I still know nothing about you. Nothing.

RICK: It could be there's nothing to know. In a way it's a relief. I want to go.

JANE: Where?

RICK: Anywhere. Back to Perth tomorrow, finish the Degree, then anywhere.

JANE: I feel so awfully sad.

RICK: Well, it's been a long time. But we had fun, didn't we? And tomorrow to fresh woods and pastures new.

JANE: Is that all you can say? You're so selfish. All you love is yourself. You're frozen inside. I can't love you because you won't let me love you!

RICK: Jane!

JANE: [*sobbing*] I hate you! Oh God, whose bloody idea was this anyway?

♦♦♦♦♦

SCENE FOURTEEN

AT ST GEORGE'S

RICK *enters with a book. He lies down on his bed and begins to read. 'And Sheep May Safely Graze' plays in the background.*

CHORUS: The university was bursting at the seams. On the green lawn of Whitfield Court young bodies decoratively dowsed in the sun and the semi-tropical garden behind Winthrop Hall was festooned with scarlet vines. Beyond the lead-lighted windows of the college, Beyond the fresh new leaves and tendrils of the virginia creeper, the river was a misty blue, flat and still.

JANE *enters.*

RICK: You know, you were just about the last person I expected to visit me at college.

JANE: Yes, I do realise that.

RICK: Well, won't you sit down? Sorry about the bed. I slept in till lunchtime, so the maid couldn't make it.

JANE: I know I shouldn't have come. Everyone stared, and a boy in a pink towel screamed and ran.

RICK: Pity you missed my room-mate. He always wears his towel round his neck.

JANE: Rick—I just wanted to see you one more time.

RICK: Well?

JANE: To say—oh damn it, that I love you, Rick.

RICK: Oh, you don't. No you don't. It was your idea to break it off.

JANE: I broke it off because—you were bored with me.

RICK: No, that's not true. But perhaps it was a relief, in some ways. I want to go.

JANE: Where?

RICK: Anywhere.

JANE: Do you really know what you want to do? Have you ever had any idea?

RICK: [*softly*] I want to be young. I don't seem to have ever had the chance. No, that's not right. I don't seem to have taken the opportunity.

JANE: Can't you be young with me?

RICK: It's been four years since Hughie and I came back from the war and, oh God, Jane, if you could imagine what sort of life we'd imagined for ourselves. Heroic lives. And what came of all that? Hughie sits in his neat little suburban house in Nedlands, listening to the wireless, and I swot for a career that bores me stiff in anticipation. And somehow, out in the big wide world, people younger than me are getting everything out of life that I promised myself that I was going to have as soon as the war stopped. I'm too young to rot. Not very young, but too young for the suburbs.

JANE: Rick, just kiss me once.

RICK: Jane, I will marry you. Marry me.

JANE: No. No, Rick. Just kiss me.

They kiss.

RICK: Oh, Jane. Oh, Jane, I've been talking a lot of rot and I do love you.

JANE: [*pushing him away*] No, you knew what you were saying.

RICK: What will you do now?

JANE: Go home. And go to work. And try to marry a doctor.

RICK: Marry me, Jane.

JANE: No. I wouldn't marry any man because he got tired of running. You got all you wanted from me, and now you know you're lovable. So keep running, Rick, and don't get caught.

JANE *turns and storms out.*

RICK: Jane, don't be so hard on me.

♦♦♦♦♦

SCENE FIFTEEN

RICK AND HUGH

RICK *crouches into the wind as he trudges along the revolve to Hugh's house.*

CHORUS: The spring storm lashed the trees, and drove the black rain into his face. The river was black and lightless, reflecting nothing, a black hole in the city, whose far lights shimmered and dimmed behind the rain.

RICK *reaches the doorway.* JOY MACKAY *greets him.*

JOY: Oh, Rick, come in.
RICK: Can I see Hughie, Joy?
JOY: Well, he's in bed.
HUGH: Is that Rick? Put him in the lounge.

There is an awkward pause.

JOY: Cool for this time of the year, isn't it?
RICK: Yes.
JOY: Oh well, Hughie will be in in a minute, so I think I'll say goodnight.
RICK: Yes, goodnight, Joy. God bless.
JOY: [*surprised*] God bless you too, Rick.

HUGH *enters in a varicoloured satin dressing-gown.*

HUGH: What's up with you?
RICK: I wanted to see you.
HUGH: I look better by daylight.
RICK: Sorry. I didn't—I didn't need to before.
HUGH: What's wrong, tell Uncle. Is it Jane?
RICK: Yes. Yes, it is.
HUGH: So. What have you done to her?
RICK: I don't know, well, yes I do. She's tried to kill herself.
HUGH: Rick, tell me more, mate.
RICK: She's not dead. She's not in danger. She's just—Oh, she took an overdose of something. These nurses can always lay their hands on anything they want. She's not going to die. But she did try.
HUGH: And how do you feel about that?

RICK: Well, how do you think I feel? I feel bloody awful. And then I think: the rotten bitch, she did it just to make me feel lousy, and I feel worse still.

HUGH: And what are you going to do about it?

RICK: Nothing. What can I do?

HUGH: And where do I come in?

RICK: Would you go and see her?

HUGH: And tell her goodbye from you?

RICK: Yeah. Something like that.

HUGH: Okay. It won't be the first time I've cleaned up after you.

RICK: Don't say it like that. As if it was my fault.

HUGH: Well…

RICK: Ah, it's no use. I can't cope with peace. I don't know where I stand. People keep asking you for things you can't give. I was a good mate to you, wasn't I, Hughie?

HUGH: Yeah, you were. But you can't live on that forever.

RICK: I wish things were as simple as that still. I feel so helpless, empty now. That need to—endure, has gone. You happy, fella?

HUGH: Mate, I worship her wet footprints on the bathmat.

RICK: Do you dream?

HUGH: Only about golf.

RICK: Ah, you insensitive ape. You lucky, lucky, moronic bastard.

HUGH: Take up golf. You'll dream about it too.

RICK *laughs and* HUGH *shakes his head.*

Well, what are you going to do now, mate?

RICK: I dunno. Leave Australia, I reckon.

HUGH: For where?

RICK: England I suppose. I don't know. But I know a fella who's got a booking on a boat for England, and I think I could talk it out of him.

HUGH: Why this mad yearning for overseas?

RICK: I'm so bloody bored. This country. It's so bloody boring.

HUGH: It could be that that's not the country's fault.

RICK: Uh-huh. Oh Jesus, Hughie, I wish you weren't wearing that dressing-gown.

HUGH: What's wrong with it?

RICK: It's bloody awful against that chair.

HUGH: Listen, Rick, if you like me, you've got to like my dressing-gown and my lounge suite and my wife and the lot.

RICK: Yeah. Hughie, I'm sorry.

HUGH: You've been on the sherbet, haven't you? Well, you better sleep here. Let's just get that tie and those shoes off.

RICK: [*trying to hug* HUGH] Oh Christ, Hughie, I think you're a bloody marvellous bloke.

HUGH: Hell, you are in the grip of the grape.

RICK: I'm not. And I'm not going to sleep here either. Funny, you know, I've only had one or two drinks but it seems to get me in the head now. I can't take it.

HUGH: Listen, mate, tell me something. You're not cracking up, are you?

RICK: I don't know. I'm dreaming again, after a couple of years of good sleep. It feels like something's going wrong.

HUGH: Why don't you marry Jane, you galah?

RICK: No, no. I couldn't face her again. I just feel so—

HUGH: Have you got any idea of what you want to do?

RICK: No. I suppose I could try kidding myself I'm a painter.

HUGH: You're a sad case. I wish I could go with you.

RICK: I wish you could, too.

HUGH: But boys grow up, and they marry girls.

RICK: That's hell, isn't it? We should have married the same woman, Hughie.

HUGH: What relation would that make us? Husbands-in-law?

RICK: Ah, you clown. Right, I feel better now. I'm going home.

HUGH: What, to Sandalwood?

RICK: No, you dope, back to college. I'll go back and say goodbye to the clan after my results are posted.

HUGH: It's going to hurt the boy.

RICK: He'll survive. *Tidak apa*, mate. Sport, we can't be worried. He's fourteen now, time he knew the facts of life.

HUGH: Which way are you going?

RICK: Ah, around by the river.

HUGH: Don't fall in.

RICK: I'm not the type. You know that.

HUGH: What type are you, though?

RICK: The type that's only got one instinct, and that's the instinct of self-preservation.

HUGH: Well, sport, goodnight and good luck, and take care of yourself.

RICK: Yeah. And give my love to your wife, 'cause I reckon she's a bonza sheila.

HUGH: She heard that, with any luck. So, happy travelling.

RICK *trudges back against the revolving stage.*

CHORUS: The wet black wind tossed the branches and Rick opened his mouth shouting without voice, feeling the stinging rain on his tongue, as he walked by the river, like a hole in the lightless city.

♦♦♦♦♦

SCENE SIXTEEN

THE FOX

ROB *walks out across the landscape.*

CHORUS: In the spring pasture at Sandalwood, and among the maturing wheat, red and blue wild geraniums flowered. By the pools and creeks the delicate mauve-petalled wild hibiscus opened, and the gold-dust of the wattles floated on water.

Walking on the small rocky hills, among the keening, flowering she-oaks, Rob knew for the first time in his life that he was young, and knew with agreeable sadness, that he would not be young for long. Time and death could stain the bright day, and the leaf-brown foxes that traced green paths in the dew could die in agony among the flowers.

ROB *contemplates a dead fox.*

Out of the tender blue sea of the lupin paddock a windmill rose, sandy-tawny with rust pinning against the lupin-blue sky. Lupins withered and foxes rotted, and the windmill whirled and whirled against all the seasons of the sky, drinking from the filled dark caves below the earth.

♦♦♦♦♦

The merry-go-round (from left): Raechelle Lee, Elizabeth Spencer, Jess Mercer, Andrew Broadbent and Kirsty Hillhouse in Black Swan Theatre Company's 2003 production. (Photo: Jurgen Lunsmann)

SCENE SEVENTEEN

THE FLAT IN MOUNT STREET

HUGH *visits* JANE *in her flat.*

JANE: It was awfully nice of you to come. But then, you are an awfully nice man.

HUGH: Everyone likes me this week, has the word got around that I'm changing my will? How d'you feel?

JANE: Angry. Ropeable.

HUGH: He's pretty cut up, you know.

JANE: I'm not angry with him. Well, yes, I am. But more with myself. What a stupid, girlish, film-starish thing to do.

HUGH: Are you still—you know—in love with him?

JANE: No. No, I don't think so. I really only worry about myself now, and what an awful embarrassment I've been.

HUGH: What do you think about him?

JANE: Goodness knows. I think I like him, in a funny sort of way. I rather hope he doesn't get married. He's more interesting as he is.

HUGH: And what about you? Will you get married?

JANE: Well, I'll have to be asked. But I think I'm the sort of girl that does get married, don't you?

HUGH: You know something? I think you're a smashing sort.

JANE: I like you too, awfully much.

HUGH: Isn't that Maplestead a lucky bugger? He's got such charming friends.

SCENE EIGHTEEN

THE POOL

CHORUS: At Ellendale pool the water by the reed-and-gum-fringed bank was almost black, green-tinged, and mirrored farther away the sudden pink cliff that reared inexplicably out of it.

ROB *strips off. He is awkward and self conscious.*

ROB: People say it's bottomless. How could anything be bottomless?

RICK: Figure of speech.

ROB: They used to tell me there was a bunyip in it, too.

RICK: Look behind you—here he comes.

ROB: What is a bunyip, Rick?

RICK: God knows. Probably some kind of fertility spirit, like the Rainbow Serpent in the Kimberleys.

ROB: It wouldn't hurt you, then?

RICK: I dunno. It might make you pregnant.

ROB: Aw.

RICK: It was a sacred place, that's certain. And I suppose the local yamidgees had the usual ideas about the spirits of the unborn children being in the water. That ring of stones, you know, that our boundary fence runs through, that could have been something to do with fertility. Hey, it's probably making new men of us, swimming here.

ROB: I am a new man.

RICK: So am I. Gone are the days when I chewed up all the hibiscus bushes around Changi to get a bit of vitamin E.

Rick riding a horse (from left): Kim Delury as Rick Maplestead, Murray Dowsett, Andrew Broadbent and Jess Mercer in Black Swan Theatre Company's 2003 production. (Photo: Jurgen Lunsmann)

ROB: Were you sterile?

RICK: Since you're rude enough to ask, yes.

ROB: Did you feel bad about it?

RICK: It didn't matter much. But hell, that's old history.

ROB: It's four years since you came home, since you wrote that bit of poetry in my book.

Thy firmness makes my circle just,
And makes me end, where I begun.

RICK: Have you worked out yet what it means?

ROB: Yeah. It means us, the family. We stayed still, and you came back. We stayed still, and you came back to where you started from.

RICK: It was more the idea. More the idea, than the fact. It was remembering you for three and a half years that kept me circling.

ROB: Were you disappointed?

RICK: I dunno. Dreams are awful glamourising things.

ROB: I dream… ugly things.

RICK: Poor kid. What, sex?

ROB: Yeah.

RICK: So does everybody, fella, don't worry.

ROB: I wish I was a kid again.

RICK: You'll have the time of your life, matey, in a few years, so think about that. Hell, I'm cold now. Shall we take in a bit of sun on the rocks?

ROB: I'd sooner get dressed.

RICK: Right, let's go. Rob—

ROB: Yeah?

RICK: You knew I was going away, didn't you?

ROB: Where?

RICK: London, to start with.

ROB: When?

RICK: A fortnight from Friday.

ROB: Rick, why?

RICK: To start living again, because I'm dying of boredom.

ROB: Oh.

RICK: That makes you sad, doesn't it?

ROB: Yeah, a bit.

RICK: Well, maybe you'll turn up on that side too, some day.

ROB: I don't want to go away. I want to stay here with you.

RICK: That sounds familiar. I think you told me that eight years ago.

ROB: All right. I know I'm not a kid now.

RICK: You are a kid. But not for much longer.

ROB *tries to hug* RICK. RICK *shrugs him off.*

Ah, fella, I don't want to fight you.

ROB: I wasn't trying to fight you—I was trying to… I'm going away, too.

RICK: You are? Where are you going?

ROB: To Guildford. In February.

RICK: Ah, well, you should like that. I did.

ROB: Is it like schools in the English boys' books?

RICK: Not really, it's more like Changi. I enjoyed it.

ROB: I'm going to wear long pants.

RICK: You're getting ancient, aren't you? Hey, is that a trace of bum fluff I see on that manly lip?

ROB: I wish I was a kid again.

RICK: What was that? Come round the other side of me.

ROB: Why?

RICK: Ah, I'm going deaf in this ear.

ROB: You can't be going deaf, you're young.

RICK: Well, they tell me I got bashed around the head by the Nips a few times too often.

ROB: Aw, Rick, you're not getting old, are you?

RICK: Don't be morbid. Hey—d'you think we ought to go?

ROB: Yeah, all right.

ROB: Heck, it's nearly 1950. Aunt Kay's nearly seventy-seven, and you're nearly twenty-nine, and… Rick, don't go.

RICK: I've got to, kid, and I've earned it.

ROB: Why do you want to go?

RICK: I want to be young before I'm old. Hell, when I was half dead in Thailand I was more alive than I am now. I had nerve-endings that I don't seem to use anymore. And I reckon that maybe, out there in the big world, I can use 'em again.

ROB: How long will you go for? When will you come back?

RICK: Never.

ROB: [*incredulously*] And leave *us*?

RICK: Look, kid, I've outgrown you. I don't want a family. I don't want a country. Families and countries are biological accidents. I've grown up and I'm on my own.

ROB: Why, what's wrong with us?

RICK: I can't stand, this—ah, this arrogant mediocrity, the shoddiness and wowserism and the smug wild-boyos in the bars. And the unspeakable bloody boredom of belonging to a country that keeps up a sort of chorus: 'Relax, mate, relax, don't make the pace too hot'. Relax, you bastard, before you get clobbered.

ROB: I thought you liked us. If you liked us, you wouldn't mind those things you're talking about.

RICK: Hell, it's Hughie's dressing-gown all over.

ROB: We always liked you. Don't you care if people like you?

RICK: Oh, kid, I know how you feel. I was your age myself. And I try to be the sort of bloke you think I am, but I'm not.

ROB: I don't know what sort of bloke I think you are.

RICK: We're being pretty honest with each other. You love me, don't you, Rob?

ROB: No, not if you're going to leave me to grow up by myself.

They mount their horses.

CHORUS: Ah, his country was pretty: spare, bare, clean-smelling country. His country was grey-green and golden under the fair-weather sky. And the blood of his country would go on and on, the blood of his country would never end and there would be Maplesteads at Sandalwood forever, and the one apostate would be forgotten.

From the high land Sandalwood stretched out like a relief map; the folds of the bare hills marked dark green with wattle, and gum.

The huge, huge land rolled out like a blanket under the world-enlarging cry of the crows, which made the screech of a snowstorm of white cockatoos in the rivergums by the creek sound busy and trivial and frail.

RICK: I think I'll let him have his head. See you at the house, kid.

ROB: Yeah.

RICK: Mate—*tidak apa*.

RICK *leaves.* ROB *is alone.*

ROB: Yeah. *Tidak apa*, mate.

CHORUS: He stared at the blue patch which was Rick, feeling bitter, uncryable tears. Rick was going, although everyone loved him. Rick was going although the boy loved him, and he had taken back the lines that he had written in the boy's book at the end of the war.

The world that the boy had believed in did not, after all, exist. The world and the clan and Australia had been a myth of his mind, and he had been, all the time, an individual.

The boy stared at the blue blur that was Rick. Over Rick's head a rusty windmill whirled and whirled. He thought of a windmill that had become a merry-go-round in a backyard, a merry-go-round that had become a substitute for another, now ruined merry-go-round, which had itself been a crude promise of another merry-go-round most perilously rooted in the sea.

THE END